Speed for Sport

Acknowledgements

- Ron Palmer
- Keiran Noonon
- Clayton Kearney
- Emma Lincoln-Smith
- Jeff Pross
- Howard Wells
- Collins Familiy
- Amanda Cartaar
- Dr Martin Lynch
- Nigel Rowden
- Phil Blake
- George Lazarou
- Darren Clarke
- Danny Aboud
- Magee Family
- Sportsmaster

Medical Disclaimer:
The exercises and advice given in this book are in no way intended as a substitute for medical advice and guidance. It is sold with the understanding that the author and publisher are not engaged in rendering medical advice. Because of the differences from individual to individual, your doctor and physical therapist should be consulted to assess whether these exercises are safe for you. Consult your doctor and physical therapist before starting this or any other exercise program. The author and publisher will not accept responsibility for injury or damage occasioned to any person as a result of participation, directly or indirectly, of the use and application of any of the contents of this book.

The Body Coach Series

Speed for Sport

Build Your Strongest Body Ever
with Australia's Body Coach®

Paul Collins

Meyer & Meyer Sports

British Library Cataloguing in Publication Data
A catalogue record for this book is available from the British Library

Paul Collins
Speed for Sport
Oxford: Meyer & Meyer Sport (UK) Ltd., 2009
ISBN 978-1-84126-261-1

Aachen, Adelaide, Auckland, Budapest, Cape Town, Graz, Indianapolis,
Maidenhead, New York, Olten (CH), Singapore, Toronto
Member of the World
Sport Publishers' Association (WSPA)
www.w-s-p-a.org

Printed and bound by: B.O.S.S Druck und Medien GmbH, Germany
ISBN 978-1-84126-261-1
E-Mail: verlag@m-m-sports.com
www.m-m-sports.com

Contents

A Word from The Body Coach®

It's a great advantage in sport to be able to move a fraction of a second more quickly than your opponent, as in many instances it determines the difference between winning and losing. Certainly some athletes are genetically gifted with speed or a high percentage of fast twitch muscles responsible for explosive muscle actions that allow them to run fast. Nonetheless, each of us has a certain percentage of fast twitch muscle fibers for explosive muscle actions and slow twitch muscle fibers for more endurance related activities that we can harness.

In order to maximize our speed potential, I have designed a **6-Stage Fastfeet® Speed for Sport™ Training Model** that incorporates a step-by-step plan of the whole training cycle an athlete undertakes at each training session. By applying the speed and technique training drills in Speed for Sport™ you will learn how to train your body to activate your fast twitch muscle fibers in order to maximise your speed potential. More importantly you will learn 6 Stages of speed development that will take you to a new level of fitness and lightning quick speed. These include:

- **Stage 1:** Pre-activity exercises
- **Stage 2:** Proper warm-up sequence including dynamic flexibility
- **Stage 3:** Main activity speed drills, skills and intervals including pure speed and equipment based agility training
- **Stage 4:** An effective cool down and stretching routines
- **Stage 5:** Recovery phases including the revolutionary Spinal Unloading Block®
- **Stage 6:** Ongoing maintenance phase for effective body management and testing throughout the year.

Whilst the body needs to train fast to be fast, it also needs phases of support that the 6-Stage Fastfeet® Speed for Sport™ Training Model offers in order to optimize overall speed potential. By improving one's knowledge and understanding of your body, together with speed, agility, reaction and quickness drills and recovery methods you create a pathway of success. This is because speed elements can be taught and developed, as running is a skill that can be learned.

Speed for Sport™ focuses on breaking down the skill of running and introducing a series of drills for improving straight, lateral and multi-directional movement patterns for the beginner and advanced. Applying these drills as part of the 6-Stage Fastfeet® Speed for Sport™ Program on a regular basis allows old habits to be broken and new one's to stick.

Incorporating proper technique and speed drills as outlined can enhance the development of power and improve biomechanical efficiency. The more biomechanically correct your body becomes, the smoother your running movements will be resulting in greater speed and efficiency as you become fitter and stronger. The more efficient you are, the less energy you use, resulting in increased ability to sustain faster speeds over set distances.

Speed for Sport™ has over 100 drills for easy referral and implementation including the revolutionary Speedhoop® speed ladder and Collins Training Method™ (CTM) focusing on the first 6-seconds of explosive movement. It also includes speed interval session examples for a total body workout that will have you coming back for more. So, no matter what sport or physical activity you are involved in, Speed for Sport™ provides the practical information required to assist athletes and coaches of all age groups and ability levels to improve speed, agility, reaction and quickness for sport.

I look forward to working with you!

Paul Collins
The Body Coach®

About the Author

Paul Collins, Australia's Personal Trainer™ is founder of The Body Coach® fitness products, books, DVD's and educational coaching systems – helping people to get fit, lose weight, look good and feel great. Coaching since age 14, Paul has personally trained world-class athletes and teams in a variety of sports from Track and Field, Squash, Rugby, Golf, Soccer and Tennis to members of the Australian World Championship Karate Team, Manly 1st Grade Rugby Union Team and members of the world-renowned Australian Olympic and Paralympic Swimming teams. Paul is an outstanding athlete is his own right, having played grade rugby league in the national competition, being an A-grade squash player, National Budokan Karate Champion and NSW State Masters Athletics Track & Field Champion.

A recipient of the prestigious 'Fitness Instructor of the Year Award' in Australia, Paul is regarded by his peers as the 'Trainers' Trainer' having educated thousands of fitness instructors and personal trainers and appearing in TV, radio and print media internationally. Over the past decade, Paul has presented to national sporting bodies including the Australian Track and Field Coaching Association, Australia Swimming Coaches and Teachers Association, Australian Rugby League, Australian Karate Federation and the Australian Fitness Industry as well as travelling to present a highly entertaining series of Corporate Health & Wellbeing Seminars for companies focused on a Body for Success™ in Life and in Business.

Paul holds a Bachelor of Physical Education degree from the Australian College of Physical Education. He is also a Certified Trainer and Assessor, Strength and Conditioning Coach with the Australian

Sports Commission and Olympic Weight Lifting Club Power Coach with the Australian Weightlifting Federation. As a Certified Personal Trainer with Fitness Australia, Paul combines over two decades of experience as a talented athlete, coach and mentor for people of all age groups and ability levels in achieving their optimum potential.

In his free time, Paul enjoys competing in track and field, travelling, food and movies. He resides in Manly Beach, Sydney, Australia

For more details visit: www.thebodycoach.com

Chapter 1
Introduction

Introduction

Speed is an important factor for success in many sports. Speed itself refers to the quickness of movement of a limb, such as the legs of a sprinter or the arms of a boxer. In this instance, the focus of this book is based on running speed across the ground in multiple directions – forwards, laterally, diagonally, angled, swerving and backwards. It also refers to first-step quickness, acceleration and reaction speed aimed at keeping you one step ahead of your competition.

The foundation for the development of speed stems back to basic movement principles. A number of training principles need to be applied and regularly practiced on an ongoing basis which form part of the Collins Training Method™ (CTM) and the revolutionary 6-Stage Fastfeet® Speed for Sport Training Model.

As general fitness levels and running technique is improved, so too is one's biomechanical efficiency, including the synergy between muscle groups, muscle fibers and the Central Nervous System (CNS) allowing a higher output of power to occur and quicker recovery after intense efforts. So, just as you practice the skills required for your sport, you also need to practice the skills as they relate to speed, agility, reaction and quickness. The goal of this program is to give you access to these drills for improving your Speed for Sport™.

Establishing a Solid Foundation

The ability to move quickly forwards, sideways, in various angles and backwards can relate to how quickly one can accelerate and decelerate whilst stabilizing the core and maintaining good muscle coordination, body awareness and balance. For this to occur, a solid core-strength and general fitness foundation is required as a starting point. This means appropriate support structures are put in place that can be built upon. In many instances, athletes may already have established this solid foundation and need to focus on improving their weaknesses through testing and evaluation for further speed improvements to occur.

Speed Variations

In team sports, rarely does an athlete run straight or reach top end speed. Compare a 100-meter sprinter with an elite soccer, rugby or tennis player and you'll notice the difference due to the multi-directional demands of each sport. For this reason, there are two initial considerations when discussing running speed.

Firstly, straight-line speed, such as the 100-meter dash, requires a high center of gravity, rapid stride frequency and optimal stride length moving rapidly in a forward direction. Secondly, multi-directional speed – change of direction, footwork, agility, acceleration, deceleration, dodging and similar movement patterns – generally require a lower center of gravity by the body. In light of this, combining a range of speed drills in multiple planes using various drills and training equipment will allow the body to develop the essential balance and coordination to assist towards sports specific speed.

In terms of the need for your sport, if your focus is solely running the 100-meter dash, the training objectives will vary to some extent to that of a team athlete who will need to develop straight line and multi-directional speed and many other variables as outlined.

Developing Speed

Developing speed involves improving the efficiency and firing of correct motor unit pathways that in turn improves the development of force in the muscle. This complex recruitment and synchronized firing of muscles involves a motor learning process that must be rehearsed at high speeds to implant the correct motor patterns. Within any muscle there are hundreds of motor units available to activate muscle contraction, depending on the type, intensity and duration of the work called for. If the motor units are switched on, then more force is produced and thus greater speed can be produced. Establishing a strong foundation through regular training intervals combined with good body management practices will enhance the wiring within these motor units and improve one's force production.

At various times in one's training progression for developing speed, some information may seem to contradict previous information and visa-versa. This is because what suits one athlete may not suit another. Drills may differ, core-strength requirements will differ, recovery periods may differ and so forth. For that reason, as part of the Collins Training Method™ (CTM) I'll soon introduce you to the Fastfeet® Training Model which plays a major role in the overall development of speed for individuals and sporting teams.

Core-Strength

Core-Strength plays an essential role towards improving sports speed and athletic performance. The body's core muscles are the foundation from which all movement occurs. The muscles of the abdominal core region help stabilize the spine and provide a solid foundation for rapid movement of the extremities. The shoulder girdle and arms provide strength and support for more powerful movements of the upper extremity. Wheress the muscles of the hip, knee and ankle allow for more efficient movement of the lower body.

Improvements in core-strength will allow better muscular synergy and movement efficiency to occur between the upper and lower extremities. The more the body's neuromuscular system begins to work as a unit, the greater benefit will arise from speed training as the body becomes more efficient. One's ability to hold and maintain a strong core throughout training or competition, without movement, enhances speed outcomes.

Essentially, all athletes will need to embark on a weekly core-strength training program to provide the essential foundational support from which all dynamic movement occurs. This includes exercises for the following muscle groups using one's own body weight and appropriate training equipment:

Note: All core-strength exercises can be utilized as tests themselves that can be improved upon, whether technique or strength. Additional exercises can be found in **The Body Coach® books – Core-Strength and Awesome Abs.**

Region	Muscle Group	Exercises and equipment
Lower Extremity	Ankle joint – Feet, Ankle, Calves Knee joint – Thigh and Hamstrings	• Body weight • Gymnastic drills • Fitness ball • Medicine ball
Core (Mid Body)	Hip joint – Gluteal region, Abdominals and Lower Back Spine – Back muscles and Abdominals	• Resistance bands • Cable machine • Balance drills • Plyometrics • Olympic Lifting • Kettle Bells
Upper Extremity	Shoulder Girdle – Upper Back, Chest and Shoulders Elbow Joint – Biceps, Triceps, forearm (wrist joint also)	

Proper Running Technique

The learning of proper running technique must be performed correctly and without fatigue present. As many athletes have never been taught the proper mechanics of running, correcting one's technique often becomes an ongoing process. By starting out with basic running drills you will learn the fundamental motor skills that lay the foundation for other skills to develop and improve. Introducing and mastering marching, for example, provides the technical aspect required for the development of speed when running at higher velocities. This is where some coaches may disagree. Hence, the angle I'm coming from here in *Speed for Sport* is to provide you with an overall understanding of what's required when working with an athlete from a beginner, intermediate, advanced and elite level. What may work for some are not required for others due to their differing skill, speed levels, core-strength and overall power output. Having an understanding of this helps one accept that all drills can play a certain role in training for some athletes and not others and should never be dismissed.

Athletes who have never been taught the technical aspects of running can benefit greatly by learning and practicing drills with good technique at both medium and high speeds. This ensures correct technique is engrained and carries over into a competitive environment. Over time if form does lapse, then general fitness and core-strength will need to be re-asessed whilst training distances may need to be shortened and progressed at a rate to which the athlete can adapt to ensure good technical transition for speed development. So, what may seem useless to an elite athlete is essential for a beginner or intermediate level athlete or child as part of their development.

Technique Progression

Training for speed is far from optimum if one's neuromuscular fibers are not developed for muscular strength, power and speed endurance. Core-strength provides joint stability whereas speed endurance provides a neuromuscular fitness base for more demanding work to be performed. This is important because speed work is performed rapidly and the body's muscles and nervous system must be able to cope during and after training week-in, week-out. So, in terms of speed progression for the beginner or intermediate athlete, running technique for speed improvement needs to be rehearsed in two phases:

(1) Moderate to fast pace (whilst learning)
(2) Transferred to runs at maximum speed without loss of form

These two phases are firstly achieved in line with general fitness improvements. Once a good foundation has been established each exercise should be performed at the highest possible intensity with good technique as anything less than maximal effort will train different neuromuscular patterns, which if done for long enough may have a negative effect on speed development. Speed work at a sports training sessions with limited time should therefore be scheduled early in the session and sprinting distances kept to a minimum to ensure good technique is maintained. Appropriate recovery periods also need to be considered.

Speed Training Drills

As muscle physiology, technical knowledge and understanding, training methods and fitness improve, more specific technical elements will arise that at times may contradict what was learnt previously. Accepting this learning curve is part of speed development. Think of learning how to run fast like starting karate classes for the first time. It takes many months of learning various techniques before being graded and able to progress to a higher belt. As you progress towards becoming a 'black belt', over many years of training, the quality improves and specific drills become instinctive.

In some cases, some athletes already have good flexibility and timing and can progress much quicker than others once they can show they are competent. Looking back from this point, the way one has been taught starts with very simple learning terms and gradually becomes more complex. This ability to break down and explain each exercise at the appropriate level for each participant is crucial. Speed for Sport™ outlines the training basics for athletes as a starting point to develop, improve and maintain speed.

Drills used to enhance Speed for Sport include, but not limited to:
- Running technique
- Foot speed drills
- Leg speed mechanics
- First-Step quickness
- Agility
- Reaction drills
- Sprinting over short distances
- Hollow sprints or 'Ins and outs'
- Core-strength
- Specific strengthening
- Towed sprinting
- Speed resistor harness or vest
- Uphill sprints
- Overspeed downhill running
- Bungee supported overspeed drills
- Bounding
- Plyometrics
- Olympic Lifting

Pure Speed versus Speed Conditioning

In working with athletes it's important to understand the difference between the concepts of **Pure Speed** and **Speed Conditioning** in order to differentiate the training methods that need to be applied throughout one's season. In simple terms, Pure Speed refers to 'quality of work' – low volume, high intensity and high quality efforts at maximum speed holding good form – where longer rest periods assist in accompanying this and workouts are performed under training conditions where athletes remain fresh and fatigue is not a factor. Overall, the goal is to develop pure sprinting speed.

On the other hand, **Speed Conditioning** focuses on 'quantity' – high volume, shorter rest period conditioning work. It can be said that Speed Conditioning is working athletes under fatigue conditions. High volume repetition sets with minimal recovery generally reflect team sports such as rugby and soccer where the actual outcome is more related to conditioning and being able to play at high intensity intervals for 80 minutes or more.

In both instances, the neuromuscular system is fatigue-prone when performing at such high intensities. With **Pure Speed**, for instance, when the quality drops it is generally time to wrap up the high quality training for the day. On the other hand, in Speed Conditioning, this is when the journey just gets started.

Fast but not Fit?

Controversy often lies in the fact that an athlete maybe fast, but not fit. By fit, I refer to the ability to perform repeated bouts at training at high velocity maintaining good form. Consequently, the training approach for a fast but not fit athlete may require shorter distance high velocity development sets. This involves establishing an athlete's speed base from shorter repeated intervals over a period of time until a quality speed base can be established maintaining good running form, then progressively increasing the running distances over weekly cycles through a periodized training model. This approach itself may contradict traditional sprint training practices of longer to shorter distances. The fact is: both training approaches will work – depending on the sporting requirements. That's why athlete testing is so important towards finding their strengths and weaknesses as well as sports specific energy requirements and applying an approach that works. Thus, with a fast but not fit athlete, training selection will depend on whether the athlete's primary focus is on explosive speed such as baseball or speed development in a team environment such as rugby.

Either way, both athletes must possess the appropriate levels of core-strength and elastic power to overcome the inertia when starting and powering forward. Both must develop a good speed endurance base so that maximum velocity can be maintained and high velocity intervals repeated, as that's what the majority of field sports ultimately require. A sport such as rugby union, for example, requires a combination of endurance, speed and power as they are played over two-halves of 40 minutes each and include physical contact. For this reason, an endurance background is extremely important towards supporting such high intensity bouts in these types of sport. With this comes the ability of the body, its muscles and Central Nervous System to handle the powerful demands placed upon it.

Energy Systems

Carbohydrates, protein and fat from the food we eat provide us with an important form of chemical energy. In order to perform physical activities, our body relies on the transformation of chemical energy from these foods into energy for muscular contraction. This energy is converted to Adenosine Triphosphate (ATP), which is stored in our muscle cells and broken down to supply our body with energy for movement. ATP is continually being used in muscular activity and resynthesized for repeated use. As ATP is stored in very small amounts, it must be constantly replenished so that activity can continue.

Essentially there are three energy systems in the human body, including:

1. **Anaerobic alactic system:** 6-10 seconds of explosive movement. For example, to improve Sports conditioning you could perform 10 x 40 meter sprints – up to 7 seconds per sprint with 28 seconds recovery (1:4 active/recovery ratio) between sprints. On the other

hand, for Pure Speed development you could work on maximal speed over distances of 20-80 meters with full recovery of up to 3 minutes or more before repeating sprinting again.

2. **Anaerobic lactic acid system:** rapid and intense activity lasting longer than 15 seconds and upwards of 1-3 minutes such as a 400m sprint. During intense exercise if your cardio-respiratory system is unable to supply oxygen quickly enough, then a waste by-product product referred to as lactic acid begins to build up in the muscles and blood causing fatigue. Tolerance to lactic acid can be improved through regular, specific training. Appropriate recovery periods in-between runs are vital for the body to recover for the next bout maintaining good form.

3. **Aerobic system:** The longer an activity lasts beyond one-minute, the greater must be the contribution of aerobic metabolism towards the total energy production necessary to meet the requirements of the activity. Although this system focuses on endurance or longer running events, I believe aerobic system training plays an important role in supporting the anaerobic alactic and lactic systems for the beginner and intermediate level athletes. I'll discuss this more in the topic Anerobic Threshold.

The sole purpose of these three energy systems is to re-synthesize ATP in order to continually provide the energy necessary for muscular contraction. The anaerobic alactic and lactic acid systems resynthesize ATP without oxygen, and are therefore termed anaerobic (i.e. without oxygen) energy systems. Whereas the aerobic system resynthesizes ATP with the use of oxygen, which is why it is termed the aerobic (i.e. with oxygen) system.

Basically all three energy systems overlap and work together to provide energy for activity. The intensity, duration and work/rest ratio determine the energy systems used during activity. Most sports require a combination of all three energy systems. For example, an elite soccer player performs repeated high intensity, short anaerobic bursts of energy for sprinting, jumping and kicking, as well as low to moderate energy requirements for jogging around the field. The overall energy contributions are approximately 30% alactic, 20% lactic and 50% aerobic – hence, the association of Speed Conditioning.

On the other hand is the Pure Speed requirement of the 100m dash which requires energy predominantly from the **anaerobic alactic system** (90% alactic and 10% lactic) for about 10 seconds for the elite level athlete. That means that a sprinter can run at full speed without needing to take a breath for about 10 seconds. For the beginner and intermediate athlete this usually means a distance of 60 to 80 meters. In addition, it will take three minutes of rest before the body is ready to repeat this type of activity again at optimal levels.

Beyond this time frame, performing high intensity intervals up to 3 minutes the body uses the **anaerobic lactic system**. This is usually for distances such as the 400 meters. Since the muscles are not getting oxygen to do the work, large amounts of lactic acid are produced causing fatigue. Hence, after a sprint for this period, runners need to walk or jog lightly to help the body remove lactic acid. Still, it may take up to sixty minutes or more for the body to get rid of all the lactic acid produced in a 400m race, depending on one's fitness levels. Beyond one minute of activity, the muscles require oxygen to continue efficiently for events such as middle and long distance running. This is called the aerobic system and is the main system we use in everyday life where oxygen is present.

Interval Training
Interval training involves alternating effort and rest times. Interval training can be used with aerobic and anaerobic energy systems. The intensity of the training determines the energy system recruited, and therefore, the time that the interval can be sustained. The nature of interval training allows a higher quality training session, because the rest allows recovery between sets so that each set can be done at a high intensity.

Active/Recovery Ratio
The Active/Recovery Ratio refers to determining the rest time taken between intervals when training the energy systems. The active time is the time to complete the interval or activity, while the rest time is the time between intervals for recovery. The table on the next page provides a brief description of the optimal Active/Recovery times for the three energy systems. The recommended recovery between intervals is referred to as active or passive rest. Active recovery refers to continuing the activity at an easy pace between the higher

The following table summarizes the energy systems and training guidelines:

Energy System	Frequency	Training Guidelines	Time	Recovery
Anaerobic Alactic System	2-3 x per week	100% effort	Intervals of 5-10 seconds focus	48 hours recovery between high intensity sessions
Anaerobic Lactic Acid System	2-3 x per week	80-85% effort	Intervals of up to 3 min	48 hours recovery between high intensity sessions
Aerobic System	In terms of speed development, the aerobic system is used to help with recovery such as tempo and technique sessions 1-2 times a week, as required	60-80% maximum	Intervals of 3-60 minutes –continuous	24 hours

intensity training. An example of active rest would be to walk or jog slowly between 400-meter intervals to help flush any lactic acid out of the muscle. On the other hand, passive recovery relates to being stationary or stretching between the intervals

Anaerobic Threshold

When an athlete performs an all out sprint that requires a great deal of power output beyond 10-seconds, the anaerobic system plays a major role. Although the energy is quickly available, the anaerobic pathways are not very efficient and short term energy stores are rapidly depleted leading to a build-up of lactic acid that interferes with performance. The intensity of effort at which the build-up of lactic acid begins to interfere with performance is termed the

Anaerobic Threshold. The Anaerobic Threshold or onset of blood lactate accumulation occurs when the lactic acid accumulation exceeds the removal.

Determining an athlete's anaerobic threshold is an important step in helping to define their required training intensity and distance before onset of lactic acid. Training below anaerobic threshold will develop primarily the aerobic energy system, while training above the anaerobic threshold will train primarily the anaerobic lactic acid system. The most important element to remember is that each athlete will vary due to age, body type, muscle fibre type, fitness level, speed capability and maximal output capabilities.

Light exercise will not cause an accumulation of lactic acid but moderate to heavy exercise will result in accumulation. It is believed that lactic acid will start to accumulate at approximately 55% of an untrained person's maximum aerobic capacity, and at approximately 80-90% of a trained person's maximum aerobic capacity.

Aerobic training will allow an athlete to train and compete at a higher percentage of their maximum aerobic capacity before they reach their anaerobic threshold. On the other hand, anaerobic training will increase the ability of athletes to generate a lot of lactic acid, as well as increasing their tolerance of a high level of lactic acid accumulation. For this reason, applying the right types of workouts is the key to properly shaping an athlete's anaerobic threshold. Regular training with this knowledge at hand can help the athletes body to remove lactate better, thus raising one's Anaerobic Threshold and performance levels.

The First Six-Seconds

In terms of speed development within the Collins Training Method™ (CTM), I'm focusing mainly on the first six-seconds of explosive movement in Speed for Sport because rarely in field sports does an explosive effort go beyond this point of time of maximum effort. In many on field sporting situations, a short explosive movement is often followed by:
- Tackling – in contact sports; whilst other team members are:
- Jogging – forwards, backwards or sideways
- Standing still – recovery periods

	Anaerobic Alactic System	Anaerobic Lactic Acid System	Aerobic System
Active/ Recovery ratio	1:10 – 1:20	1:3 – 1:5 Note: Ratios will vary if aiming for lactate accumulation (ie. 2:1)	2:1 1:1
Sport-specific	• Sprint 6-seconds before repeating • 10 plyometric jumps in 6 sec; and rest 60 sec before repeating.	• Shuttle runs (30-45 sec): rest for 90 sec before repeating. • Training drills lasting 4 min; rest 2-minutes before repeating (lactate accumulation).	• 1km run in 4 min followed by 2-min rest before repeating.
Recommended recovery between intervals	Passive (e.g. stretch between plyometric jump intervals).	Active (e.g. easy jog between the shuttle runs).	Active (e.g. run four mins, walk for two mins).

As I've discussed previously, in terms of improving speed conditioning, the heart rate will remain high after the initial six-seconds and short recovery periods are designed to imitate on-field simulations for anaerobic speed conditioning for team sports. Although, in terms of pure speed development, after an all-out explosive effort is performed, much longer periods of recovery are required in order for the body to recover completely for the next effort. So, whatever your goals, be warm and be ready to explode for six-seconds and over time you can build from here.

Speed Development Summary Points

The following outlines key points as part of your **Speed for Sport** program:

- Perform pre-activity Stage 1 Drills.

- Ensure an appropriate dynamic warm-up is performed at each session as part of Stage 2 drills.

- Focus on the first six-seconds of explosive movement at maximum effort.

- Duration of work 1–8 seconds for pure speed development and 8–30 seconds or more for speed conditioning .

- Duration of recovery for speed various in terms of active-recovery ratio. The higher the ratio of recovery the higher the quality of movement being performed. In some instances, this may incur 30–180 seconds before repeating for fitness purposes or up to 10 minutes or more recovery for an elite athlete sprinting at maximal speed performing pure speed specific interval sets.

- Aim to complete each specific main activity (Stage 3) drill in the shortest possible time whilst maintaining good technique throughout whole movement pattern.

- The emphasis for speed development is on quality, not quantity. When the quality of the sprint efforts decline, speed training should come to an end.

- Any new drill or activity has to be demonstrated, taught, practiced, assessed and mastered.

- It is important that flexibility and range of motion of muscles and joints is maintained all year round.

- Speed for sport utilizing multi-directional changes requires a lower center of gravity than pure sprinting (ie. 100m dash).

- Core-strength exercises are important for the development of good posture, muscle tone and decreasing body fat levels. Ensure an equate core-strength base is acquired before attempting more dynamic drills such as plyometrics.

- Always cool-down and stretch to conclude a session (Stage 4).

- During the week, specific speed training should be limited to two (or three) sessions with at least 48 hours recovery to allow the central nervous system to recover. In between, tempo and core-strength training can be applied.

- Tempo work is performed up to 75% of maximum effort in-between sprint sessions, having a higher focus on quantity in terms of fitness and technique.

- In order to maximize speed development, regular stretching, massage, range of movement, good nutrition and other body regeneration methods are required on an ongoing basis to keep the body fresh – see Stages 5 and 6 of the Fastfeet® Speed Training Model.

- The development of a yearly training plan with the appropriate macro, meso-and-micro-cycles is essential for the development and maintenance of speed in Stage 6.

Chapter 2

Stage 1: Pre-Activity

Fastfeet® Speed for Sport Training Model

In order to work towards positive speed development outcomes I have developed the Fastfeet® Speed for Sport Training Model as part of the Collins Training Method™ (CTM) incorporating six stages. The objective is to provide you with a basic training model to help you maximize your speed potential. Each stage has its own unique application in the development of lightning quick speed.

In some cases, an athlete may simply be missing one stage as part of their current training program and by simply incorporating this stage into their training see vast improvements. On the other hand, other athletes will benefit from introducing all six stages as part of their ongoing development. Either way, my goal is to provide you with a training model that includes exercises and drills to help you achieve your speed development goals as part of an ongoing athletic training cycle. Over the upcoming chapters, I will expand upon the Fastfeet® Speed for Sport Training Model to help you apply these various stages of the training cycle.

6-Stage sequence of a training session may consist of the following breakdown of time:

Training Sequence	Time
Stage 1a: Passive Muscle Assessment (PMA)	5-10 minutes
Stage 1b: Pre-activity Range of Motion (PROM)	5-10 minutes
Stage 2: Warm-up	10-20 minutes
Stage 3: Main Workout Session including recovery periods	30-60 minutes
Stage 4: Cool Down and Stretching	10-20 minutes
Stage 5: Recovery	Recovery principles start at the conclusion of stage 4 over an extended period
Stage 6: Maintenance	Period between end of one training session and start of the next one

Fastfeet® Speed for Sport Training Model

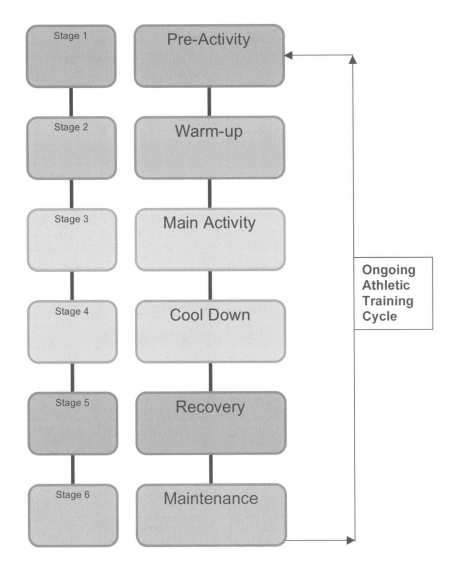

Stage 1	Pre-Activity
Stage 2	Warm-up
Stage 3	Main Activity
Stage 4	Cool Down
Stage 5	Recovery
Stage 6	Maintenance

Ongoing Athletic Training Cycle

Stage 1: Pre-Activity

Pre-activity drills incorporate actions that will bring awareness of your body and its muscles and joints

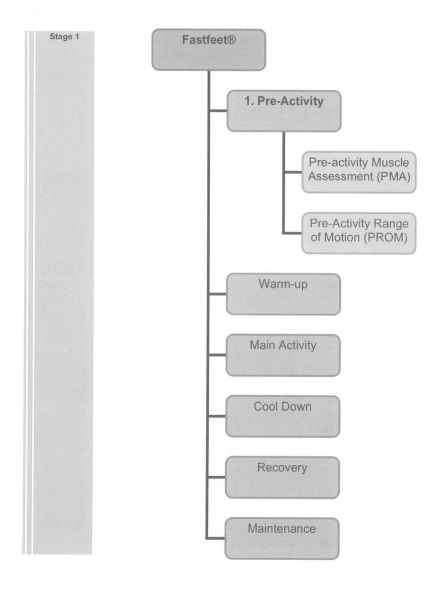

Stage 1

Fastfeet®

1. Pre-Activity

Pre-activity Muscle Assessment (PMA)

Pre-Activity Range of Motion (PROM)

Warm-up

Main Activity

Cool Down

Recovery

Maintenance

1a. Passive Muscle Assessment (PMA)

Passive Muscle Assessment or PMA plays a significant role in monitoring muscular tension from the demands of exercise, sport and daily lifestyle. Tension itself builds within our muscular framework from the gravitational forces placed on our body, whether through physical activity or a stationary position such as sitting down operating a computer. Many people are unaware of this latent build up of tension occurring over years like a silent time bomb. In some cases symptoms of pain arise out of nowhere causing tension, muscle weakness, a limited range of movement and even reduced athletic performance. Whichever the case, it is recommended that regular monthly muscular-skeletal check-ups and adjustments be made by a certified physical therapist or osteopath to help manage one's musculoskeletal framework, especially when exercising or playing sport on a regular basis.

In the meantime, PMA serves as a valuable way for athletes to pinpoint muscular tension throughout the body. The term 'Passive' refers to muscles being tested without function or activity, generally in a lying position using a muscle gauge and release tool known as The Body Coach® Muscle Release Tool (MRT). Emulating a clenched fist often used by an osteopath to gauge and release muscular tension areas when working on their clients, The Body Coach® Muscle Release Tool (MRT) can be used on the following areas to gauge, assess and help release muscular tension allowing you to communicate with your body. Below are a series of PMA exercises:

Passive Muscle Assessment (PMA)
- Have a warm shower and gentle stretch within shower prior to all sporting activity
- Always place MRT on muscle, never on bone
- Position under muscle and gently add pressure with bodyweight
- Hold position without pain for 5-30 seconds
- Relocate body position using small increments around area specified

1. Gluteal Region

Description

Lie on back and roll legs to the side. Place Muscle Release Tool under upper portion of gluteal (butt) region. Roll legs back over to increase pressure and help release any tension. Using small incremental movements, work around whole gluteal region on left and right sides to help gauge and release muscular tension.

2. Piriformis

Description

Sit up with hands behind the back and roll legs to the side. Place Muscle Release Tool under mid buttock region and roll legs back over to increase load. Using small incremental movements, work around whole gluteal region on left and right sides to gauge and release tension.

3. Shoulder Girdle

Description

Place Muscle Release Tool on floor with knob upwards. Position body on Muscle Release Tool between spine and shoulder blade on muscle (never bone). Roll body back across to feel pressure. Release and relocate by moving body. Work up and around shoulder blade on both sides to gauge and release tension. Extend arm overhead or raise hips to increase load on muscle group.

4. Lower Back

Description

Place Place Muscle Release on floor with knob upwards. Position Muscle Release Tool on erector spinae muscle. Gently pull knee in towards chest to increase pressure. Release and relocate by moving body. Work up spinal muscles on left and right sides to gauge and release tension.

5. Calf and Shin Region

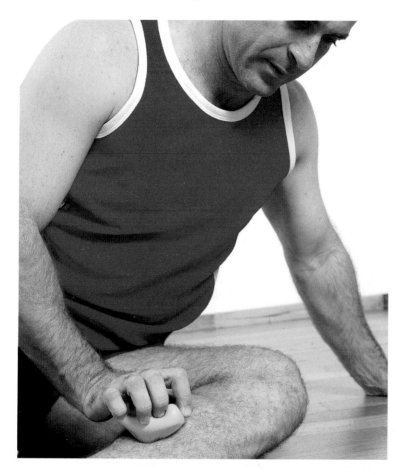

Description

Using large knob, gently push Muscle Release Tool into calf region to gauge muscular tension. Push, hold, release at regular intervals along the inner calf region. Perform on left and right leg.

In addition, apply massage oil or Vitamin E cream to lower leg and run both thumbs down the inner calf region to help release muscular tension and use a similar approach to the tibialis anterior.

For more information on the Body Coach® Muscle Release Tool (MRT) visit: www.thebodycoach.com

1b. Pre-activity Range of Motion (PROM)

Pre-activity Range of Motion (PROM) is a preliminary series of low-intensity exercises performed after a Passive Muscle Assessment (PMA) and prior to a Dynamic Warm-up. In many instances, athletes who arrive early to training may perform these drills whilst waiting. These drills provide a long-term benefit for athletes by helping progressively introduce range of motion drills for each joint, bringing body (spatial) awareness, pinpointing any musculoskeletal tension that may require extra attention whilst kick-starting the nervous system into action for the Dynamic warm-up that soon follows.

Performing Range of Motion drills is like an airline pilot checking over the plane and all controls prior to take-off. The aim is to bring attention to details of oneself and how the body is functioning. The application of these drills means that during a dynamic warm-up the athlete will become more conscious of performing each drill with correct technique leading to improved performance.

Balance, posture, coordination and range of motion drills are used at a low-intensity and slow to moderate pace. Ensure good posture from head to toe is applied along with deep rhythmical breathing. The number of sets and repetitions are also kept low, as they are not focused on strength gains but muscle and body control leading into a Dynamic Warm-up. Additional light activity sports drills such as passing a rugby ball between two people at different angles and sides of the body is also a great way to increase range of motion without excess stress of the body in these early stages. Where kicking a football too rapidly or dynamically when the body is cold and without properly warming up may be counterproductive and lead to injury

**The following drills may be utilized as part of a
Pre-activity Range of Motion Routine (PROM)**

Twist Left

PROM1: Hip and Spine Mobility

Description
- Stand tall with feet parallel and hands at chest height.
- Breathing out, twist the body and arms in a flowing motion to the left side, rotating on the ball of the feet. Repeat across to the right side.
- 10 twists across to each side.

Twist Right

Balance on one foot

PROM2: Balance Calf Raise

Description
- Stand tall with hands on hips and raise one knee up with thigh parallel to ground.
- Raise up onto toes, then lower.
- Repeat 10 repetitions each leg.

Rise up onto toes

Start

PROM3: Body Weight Squats

Description
- Stand tall with feet shoulder-width apart and arms extended forward in front of the body parallel to ground.
- Lower body slowly by simultaneously bending at the hip, knee and ankle region.
- Keep knee alignment over middle toes and sustain solid foot arch to avoid rolling knees in and lifting heels.
- Repeat 8-12 times.

Lowered

Start

PROM4: Stationary Lunge

Description
- Stand tall with one foot forward and leg slightly bent and the other foot back, leg straight and resting up on toes. Place hands on hips.
- Lower and raise body by simultaneously bending front and rear knee towards ground then rising.
- Repeat both sides 8-12 times (each leg).

Lowered

THE BODY COACH

PROM5: Single Leg Balance

Starting position

Description
- Stand tall with feet together, hands on hips and abdominal muscles braced.
- Extend one leg backwards until torso is parallel to ground. Use arms for balance and keep hips square.
- Hold briefly (1-5 seconds) and return to starting position.
- Perform 5 times on each leg.

Raised Position

Start with arms by side

PROM6: Star Jumps

Description
- Stand tall with feet together and arms by your side.
- Simultaneously raise arms up overhead whilst jumping legs out wide, then back together to complete start jump movement.
- Repeat 8-10 times.

Mid-point: Arms and legs wide

PROM7: Lateral Leg Lifts

Lie on side

Raise upper leg, keeping heel up high

Description

- Lie on side of body with lower leg bent at hip and knee and head resting against extended lower arm. Upper arm is forward of the body with hand on ground supporting body weight.
- With toes dorsi-flexed raise and lower upper leg keeping the heel as the highest point at all times.
- Repeat 10-15 times each leg.

PROM8: Push-ups

Rest on knees and hands

Midpoint: Lower chest to ground

Description

- Lie on ground in front support position with hands shoulder width apart body extended resting on toes with feet together.
- Keeping arms against body, bend elbows and lower and raise body.
- Repeat 6-12 times.

Note: perform on knees as lower intensity drill

THE BODY COACH

PROM9: Abdominal Slide

Start | Mid-point: Slide hands to knees

Description

- To activate abdominal muscles that help support the spine, lie on your back with knees bent and rest hands on thighs.
- Contracting abdominal muscles simultaneously slide hands up thighs until palms reach knees, then lower.
- Repeat 8-12 times.

PROM10: Lower Abdominal Leg Lifts

Start | Lifting hips off ground

Description

- Lie on your back with hands under buttock and legs raised vertically though slightly bent
- Activating lower abdominal muscles, lift hips off ground raising legs up into the air, without swinging legs, then lower.
- Repeat 8-12 times.

Chapter 3

Stage 2: Warm-up

Stage 2: Warm-up

As the scientific knowledge and understanding of our body and training practices improve, an effective warm-up plays a number of crucial roles towards improving athletic performance and should precede any fast, powerful explosive sprinting movements. The objectives of Stage 2 include:

- Gradually increase your heart rate and core body temperature by performing activities on the move.
- Set in motion your muscular and nervous systems.
- Work muscles and joints through an appropriate range of movement.
- Heighten the ability of your muscles to contract and be ready for activities that follow reducing the risk of injury.
- Allow you to warm up your muscles so that they are ready to work at full speed.
- Improve physical and mental alertness by setting a tone to follow for the rest of the session.
- Incorporates a routine of exercises to improve balance, technique, coordination and range of movement.
- Improve athleticism, running form and flexibility.

For the coach, an effective warm-up helps create a positive environment for the whole training session by establishing workable boundaries and athlete task focus for the training or competition that follows. Drills utilized need to adapted to suit one's age, skill and ability levels.

Stage 2: Warm-up – Individual or Team

The warm-up consists of 3-specific phases to ensure the body is ready for the more dynamic speed work that follows:

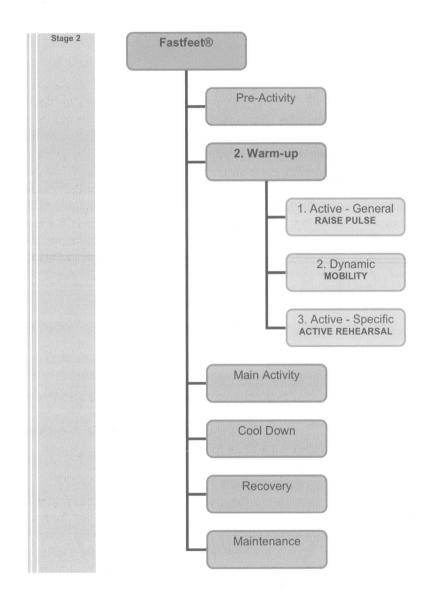

THE BODY COACH

1. Active – General

The Active - General phase of a warm-up is designed to gradually increase the heart rate by performing low-level physical activities and drills as an individual or group. This may include light jogging, submaximal running drills, group activities or games. The actual type, often depend on the training age and skill level of the athlete or team.

In terms of developing speed for sport, the Active - General warm-up is a great time to focus on improving Basic Running Technique (BRT). Basic Running Technique aims to improve body posture, hip position, leg and arm action, rate of hip extension and speed of limb recovery after push off. The length of your running stride affects how much distance you gain with each stride taken. If a person can improve their stride length by just a few centimeters and maintain their stride frequency, the individual will improve speed. For example, more distance is gained in the same number of steps (or frequency), which in turn, means that the individual will cover more ground faster than with the shorter stride length. Learning Basic Running Technique therefore provides the foundation for this to occur and should be practiced regularly all year round.

Consider the following points when assessing your running technique:

Area of body	Correct Running Form
Head	The head should be erect, with eyes focused forward.
Shoulders	The shoulders should be square and level without swinging them forwards or backwards.
Arms	Elbows should be bent approximately 90 degrees with forearms remaining roughly parallel to the ground. Arms should be swinging freely in a forward and backwards motion from waist to chin – not across the body.
Hands	Hands are held in a relaxed fist with the thumb resting on the forefinger with the wrists straight.
Torso or abdominal region	The body should be tall, with torso long and erect, chest up, and stomach braced.

(Note: Additional strength exercises will be required to keep this area of the body strong)

Hips	The hips should remain square with no sideways movement
Legs	Acceleration of the thigh on both upward and downward movements. An active plant with lower leg – downward and backward claw with thigh and lower leg. Tight and active heel recovery following push-off.
Feet	The feet should be pointed straight ahead and land directly under the hips on ball of foot for a short period

The following Basic Running Technique (BRT) drills may include stationary, forwards, sideways, diagonal and backwards variations. Drills can be performed in a series of sets with specific amount of repetitions, set time or distance travelled depending on the activity and warm-up requirements.

BRT1: Stationary Arm Swings

Swing arms using running action

Repeat arm swings opposite side

Emphasis
- Increase core-shoulder temperature and improve arm action for running technique.

Description
- Stand tall with feet shoulder-width apart and arms bent at 90-degrees at the elbow.
- Maintaining square shoulder, swing the arms forward and back in a sprinting motion.

Teaching Points
- Gently place thumb against index finger.
- Keep hands relaxed but wrists straight.
- Keep elbows at 90-degrees at all times.
- Maintain relaxed shoulders and look forward.
- Swing arms forwards and back without crossing the body.
- Arms should brush the body as they raise from waist to chin.
- Gradually increase the speed of movement.
- Maintain focus and good body alignment until repetitions are completed.
- Sustain deep breathing rhythm.

Note: The coach can stand behind athlete with their hands raised allowing the elbows to touch the hands when swinging back to ensure good range of motion

BRT2: Seated Arm Swings

Sit with toes dorsi-flexed   **Swing arms using running action**

Emphasis
- Increase core-shoulder temperature and improve arm action for running technique.

Description
- Sit on ground with legs extended forward and slightly bent, resting on heels with toes dorsi-flexed.
- Keep torso erect with arms bent at 90-degrees.
- Maintaining square shoulders swing the arms forward and back in a sprinting motion.

Teaching Points
- Gently place thumb against index finger.
- Keep hands relaxed but wrists straight .
- Keep elbows at 90-degrees at all times.
- Maintain relaxed shoulders and look forward.
- Swing arms forwards and back without touching the ground or crossing the body.
- Arms should brush the body as they raise from waist to chin.
- Gradually increase the speed of movement without losing form.
- Maintain focus and good body alignment until repetitions are completed.
- Sustain deep breathing rhythm.

BRT3: Dorsiflexion of Foot

Point toes   **Flex toes towards shins**

Emphasis
- Promote foot awareness in running.

Description
- Stand tall with hands on hips and extend one leg forward a few inches off the ground with toes pointed.
- Dorsi-flex toes back towards shin and hold. Point and Flex.

Teaching Points
- Maintain square hips at all times.
- Keep weight on balance leg across 'foot print'.
- Point and flex foot to grasp muscle action and correct foot position.
- Look forward with chest held tall and head in neutral position.
- Maintain focus and good body alignment.
- Repeat with opposite leg forward.

BRT4: Walking on Feet

Walk forwards on balls of feet

Walk forwards with toes turned inwards

Walk forwards with toes turned outwards

Walk on heels

Emphasis

- Increase foot/ground proprioceptive awareness, balance and coordination.
- Teach the importance of running fast on the ball of the feet by being aware of the most efficient movement pattern and foot position.

Description

- Stand tall with hands on hips (or running motion):
- Walk on Ball of Feet with Toes Pointing Forwards
- Walk on Ball of Feet with Toes Turned Inwards
- Walk on Ball of Feet with Toes Turned Outwards
- Walk on Heels
- Walk forwards, sideways and backwards
  (repeat foot action a–d)

THE BODY COACH

BRT5: Single Foot Hop

Leg raised   **Small hop off ground on same leg**

Emphasis
- Improve foot, ankle and calf strength and coordination

Description
- Stand tall on one leg with the other leg bent and hands forward of the body in a ready position.
- Using small hops, jump and land on ball of foot
- Repeat on opposite leg

Teaching Points
- Work off balls of feet in a stationary position
- Perform small fast hops only
- Gradually increase the speed of movement without loss of form
- Maintain focus and good body alignment and strong torso
- Repeat with opposite leg

Variation
- Single Foot Hop in forward direction using small, yet fast hops
- Single Foot Hop backwards and laterally (leading and rear leg)

BRT6: Double Foot Hop (Bouncing)

Stand tall in starting position   **Spring off toes keeping legs straight**

Emphasis
- Improve foot, ankle and calf strength and coordination.

Description
- Stand tall with hands on waist and hop up and down on the ball of the feet, on the spot, using both feet simultaneously.

Teaching Points
- Gently brace abdominal muscles and hold.
- Work off balls of feet in a stationary position keeping legs straight.
- Perform only small fast hops – bouncing not jumping.
- Gradually increase the speed of movement without loss of form.
- Maintain focus and good body alignment and strong torso.

Variation
- Double Foot Hop in forward direction using small, yet fast hops.
- Double Foot Hop backwards and laterally.

BRT7: Clawing

1. Raise knee   **2. Claw foot down**   **3. Recovery**   **4. Return to high knee position**

Emphasis
- Promote correct foot position and leg action in running.

Description
- Stand tall and raise one knee until thigh parallel to ground – toes dorsi-flexed.
- Cycle (claw or paw) raised leg down and back up in a running action.
- Maintain stationary position.

Teaching Points
- Maintain square hips at all times.
- Look forward with chest held tall and head in neutral position.
- Maintain dorsiflexion of foot at all times to avoid toes dropping.
- Claw ground and bring heel towards buttock with thigh once again parallel to ground.
- Avoid reaching foot forward in claw cycle, use piston leg action.
- Gradually increase the speed of movement without loss of form, especially foot position.
- Maintain focus and good body alignment until repetitions completed.
- Hold onto wall or partner for balance, when first beginning.
- Raise onto ball of foot of support leg to challenge body balance.
- Repeat with opposite leg.

BRT8: Ankling

Right foot action   **Left foot action**

Emphasis
- Improve foot speed and coordination.

Description
- Moving forwards, step foot over foot with fast ground contact and low foot recovery, landing and pushing off the ball of the foot.

Teaching Points
- Land and push-off the ball of your feet.
- Emphasise plantar flexion phase of ground contact.
- Perform fast small foot movements.
- Minimise ground contact, keeping light on feet.
- Gradually increase the speed of movement without loss of form.
- Maintain focus and good body alignment and strong torso.

Variation
- Increase foot speed and/or knee lift.
- Perform backwards.

THE BODY COACH

2. Dynamic Mobility
(i) Basic Dynamic Warm-up Drills (BDW)

The Basic Dynamic Warm-up is designed on a progression of low to moderate intensity drills performed at a slow to moderate pace. The objective is increasing the body's core temperature whilst taking muscles and joints through a range of motion. Speed is therefore kept to a minimum. Once a dynamic warm-up is completed more intense and specific running technique and agility drills that place a higher stress on the body may be introduced.

Following are a series of basic dynamic warm-up drills put into a sequence. Overtime and experience you may find more specific drills you can adapt that suit the needs of your sport or your body. A Basic Dynamic Warm-up (BDW) is a great way to get started.

Initial Warm-up Movements may include:
1   2 x 40-meter easy stride throughs at 50% of maximum.
2   Stride Backwards 40-meters at 50% of maximum.
3   Stride Forwards changing directions for 40-meters at 50% of maximum.
4   Repeat the above three drills at 75% of maximum.

BDW1: Side Shuffle

1. Legs together
2. Step to side

Emphasis
- Promote hip, gluteal, adductor, thigh and hamstring core temperature.

Description
- Stand tall, feet together and hands on waist in lateral position to direction of travel.
- Step laterally wide to the side and squat.
- Bring both feet together and then repeat side shuffle step again over set distance.
- Repeat action in opposite direction, leading with the opposite leg.

Variation
- Rotate 180-degrees with each side shuffle when moving forwards.

BDW2: Walking Lunge

1. Lunge left leg forward

2. Lunge right leg forward

Emphasis
- Improve leg and hip balance, strength, flexibility and coordination for increasing stride length and maintaining a full range of movement.

Description
- Stand tall with feet together and hands on hips.
- In a flowing motion lunge forward with erect torso until both legs reach approximately 90-degree angle before repeating action leading with opposite leg over set distance:
    - Option A: Lunge forward with hands on hips.
    - Option B: Lunge forward and twist arms across body.

Variation
- Repeat movements (a) and (b) in backwards motion.

BDW3: Side Skip

1. Cross arms

2. Side Skip and raise arms

Emphasis
- Promote lateral hip stabilizers and core temperature.

Description
- Stand tall, feet together and arms by your side.
- Stepping laterally skip leg wide.
- Bring both feet together and then repeat side skip again.
- Continue momentum of lateral skip with feet apart and feet together over set distance.
- Repeat action in opposite direction, leading with the opposite leg.

Variation
- Raise arm parallel to ground and hold whilst feet skip under you.

BDW4: Carioca Cross-overs

1. Arms raised

2. Legs cross behind, then in-front

Emphasis
- Promote correct foot and leg action in lateral movement.

Description
- Stand tall, feet together and hands raised parallel to ground.
- The rear (trailing) leg crosses in front of the body in a lateral motion.
- Step out wide again – legs apart.
- Continue lateral movement crossing the training leg behind the body.
- Step out wide again – legs apart – and repeat cycle.
- Repeat action in opposite direction with new lead foot when sequence completed.

Variation
- Add high knee drive across the body from the rear (trailing) leg with every cycle.

BDW5: Forward Skip Arm Cross

1. Skip and cross arms

2. Skip and open arms

Emphasis
- Promote increase in body temperature.

Description
- Move forwards in a forward skipping motion crossing arms in-front of the body and out wide.
- Cross and expand arms in time with forward skipping motion.
- Keep head upright and neutral whilst maintaining strong core posture.

Variation
- Perform travelling backwards.
- Perform raising arms up and down in front of the body.

THE BODY COACH

BDW6: Butt Kicks

1. Kick butt with heel

2. Bring heel to buttock

Emphasis
- Promote hamstring core temperature.

Description
- Move forwards with a rapid leg heel kicking action towards the buttocks (gluteal region).
- Ensure normal upright running posture is maintained as well as arm drive .
- Keep leg action rapid and steps short so as to emphasise short fast movements.

Variation
- 10m fast, 10m jog, 10m fast.

BDW7: Stiff-leg Runs

1. Lunge left leg forward   2. Lunge right leg forwards

Emphasis
- Promote hamstring core temperature and ankle activation.

Description
- Working off the balls of the feet, move forwards keeping legs straight.
- Stay tall with hips remaining square and upper body slightly leaning forwards.
- Drive arms with alternate leg movement.
- Gradually increase the speed of movement without loss of form.

Variation
- Rapid leg movements at low leg height for 10m before increasing drive up to knee height for 10m.
- Fast and short and fast and long leg drive.

BDW8: High Skips

1. Lunge left leg forward
2. Lunge right leg forwards

Emphasis
- Promote high knee action, hip extension and hamstring activation

Description
- Move forwards in marching pattern jump high off ground with very high knee action.
- Land and repeat high knee movement with opposite leg.
- Include high running action with arms.
- Maintain focus and good body alignment until repetitions completed.
- Gradually increase the speed of movement without loss of form.

Variation
- Drive both arms up into the air whilst driving forwards.

BDW9: Walking Knee Hugs

1. Lunge left leg forward
2. Lunge right leg forwards

Emphasis
- Promote range of movement and hip flexibility.

Description
- Standing tall, march forwards raising thigh up until parallel to ground, before grasping knee with both hands and gently pulling inwards towards stomach.
- Release and repeat drill with opposite leg whilst stepping forwards.
- Look forwards with chest held tall and head in neutral position.
- Raise high up on toes whilst pulling knee into stomach.
- Gradually increase the speed of movement without loss of form.

Variation
- Pull to chest, step 1-2-3 and repeat on opposite leg.

Dynamic Mobility
(ii) Dynamic Stretches (DS)

The second part of dynamic mobility involves performing a series dynamic stretches briefly for the hip, lower back and leg regions to assist towards ensuring optimal range of motion is achieved.

The post warm-up stretches may include:

DS1: Dynamic Lateral Leg Swing

Using agility pole, wall, fence or partner for support, rise up onto ball of foot and swing leg laterally out to side and down in front of opposite leg. Swing across 8 –12 times. Repeat on opposite side.

DS2: Dynamic Forward and Back Leg Swing

Using agility pole, wall, fence or partner for support, rise up onto ball of foot and swing leg forward and back without arching lower back. Keep abdominals braced. Swing forward and back 8 –12 times. Repeat on opposite side.

DS3: Calves

In a front support position, rest one foot on top of the other. Resting on toes, gently press heel to the floor. Hold 3 seconds then gently bounce on toes for 3-seconds. Repeat on opposite leg

DS4: Touch Backs

Lie on stomach on ground with arms wide. Rotate right leg back across body towards ground. Roll back to middle and repeat drill by crossing left leg across body towards ground. Complete this drill in a flowing motion from left to right sides 5-10 times.

DS5: Crosses

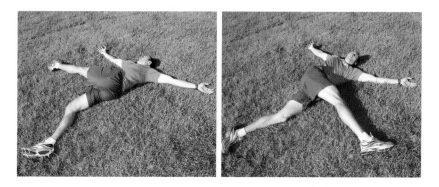

Lie on back with arms outstretched at shoulder height and left leg across body touching ground on right side. Breathing out, draw left leg back across to the midline of the body whilst simultaneously changing legs and taking the right leg across to the left side. Complete this drill in a flowing motion from left to right sides 5-10 times.

3. Active Specific

This period of a warm-up brings in specific skills related to each sport. It may start with high intensity sprints over a short distance then progress onto specific movements that imitate game play – running forwards, sideways, laterally and backwards. In teams ball sports it may include running, kicking, jumping and catching before progressing further into team rehearsal of drills. For instance, rugby backline movements or simulated team run through.

Coach Collins warming up professional rugby league team with active specific ball skills and team-specific game simulation drills

Chapter 4

Stage 3: Main Activity

Stage 3: Main Activity

The main activity in Speed for Sport™ relates to specific drills, skills, activities and training equipment used in developing speed. The initial focus here is based on the first six-seconds of explosive movement and Pure Speed where fatigue and lactic acid build-up is avoided. Fatigue itself is often prevented if an Active-Recovery Ratio of 1:10- 1:20 or up to 3-minutes recovery is used in high intensity pure speed drills where the body needs to be fully recovered for speed improvement. On the other hand, when the goal is speed conditioning, the recovery periods are reduced considerably as the body adapts to the repetitive speed interval requirements and lactic acid build up for improved tolerance when competing in sport.

The following Main Activity Speed training drills are layered in multiple sections over the upcoming chapters:

1. First-Step Quickness and Agility (FSQA)
2. Reaction Drills (RD)
3. Specific Running Drills (SRD)
4. Mini-Hurdles Drills (MHD)
5. Speed Ladder (SL)
6. Line Hops (LH)
7. Medicine Ball Power Drills (MBPD)
8. Plyometric Drills (PD)
9. Multi-Directional Speed Training (MDST)
10. Resisted Running (RR) and Overspeed Training (OT)
11. Speed Training Interval Sessions
12. Testing – Speed, Agility and Power

Stage 3: Main Activity – Speed Training

The main activity in Speed for Sport relates to specific drills, skills, activities and training equipment used for speed improvement

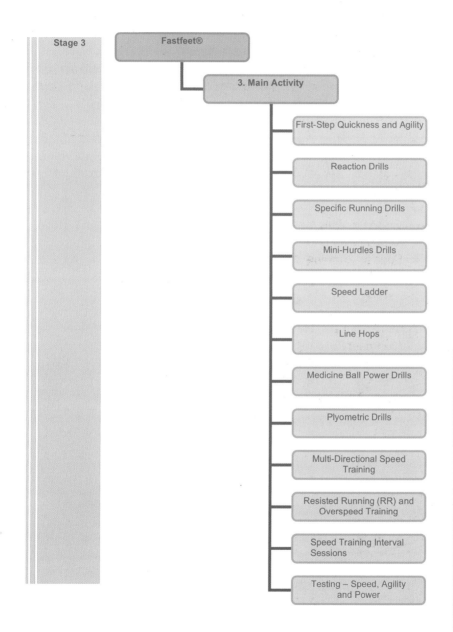

Stage 3

Fastfeet®

3. Main Activity

First-Step Quickness and Agility

Reaction Drills

Specific Running Drills

Mini-Hurdles Drills

Speed Ladder

Line Hops

Medicine Ball Power Drills

Plyometric Drills

Multi-Directional Speed Training

Resisted Running (RR) and Overspeed Training

Speed Training Interval Sessions

Testing – Speed, Agility and Power

First Step Quickness and Agility (FSQA)

First Step Quickness is the ability to move the body quickly from a stationary or moving position, where agility is the ability to change the direction of the body in an efficient and effective manner. Combining these two key elements together, you create a combination for speed improvements to occur.

In sport, having first step quickness may mean all the difference in beating a defender or reaching a ball first. Applying the drills outlined in the previous chapters is essential for one's neuromuscular development and explosive response. Synergy between the upper and lower body is progressively developed through each chapter in this book. As body posture, balance, coordination, timing and fitness improve so to does the body's neurological capacity to respond and recover quicker.

The following drills aims to improve one's ability to respond quicker and should be performed at maximal speed after an appropriate warm-up:

FSQA1: Falling Starts

1. Stand tall
2. Raise onto toes and lean forward
3. React, land and sprint forwards

Emphasis
- Improve leg reaction, drive and acceleration.

Description
- Stand tall with feet together and hands by your side.
- Lean forward and raise up onto toes until balance is lost.
- React with two quick steps and rapid arm drive followed by short sprint over 10-20m.

Teaching Points
- Look forward with chest held tall and head in neutral position.
- Lean and react with arm drive and two-quick steps.
- Maintain strong core and upright posture.
- Continue good body mechanics for short sprint.

Variation
- After two-steps and short sprint add change of direction – left or right.
- Add decision after short sprint – ie. dodge, weave or step.
- START and STOP – falling start, sprint 10m and stop.
  Repeat 4 times.

FSQA2: Side Stepping – Zigzag

Run forwards

Step off left foot

Emphasis
- Improve lateral strength and movement of each leg.

Description
- Start off with running motion in a forward direction, then plant left foot and step to the right, then right foot and step to the left.
- Continue this action for set distance.

Teaching Points
- Work off the balls of the feet as you transfer weight forward and diagonally.
- The step force should be equal on both legs.
- Sustain deep breathing rhythm.
- Gradually increase the speed of movement without loss of form.

THE BODY COACH

FSQA3: Knee-out Steps

Emphasis
- Improve leg reaction, drive and acceleration in opposite direction.

Description
- Stand tall in ready position.
- On coach's call to your right – lift right knee up and rotate out and backwards behind your body turning on the ball of your feet.
- Whilst rotating 180-degrees lean body into direction of travel – opposite direction of starting point.
- React with short sprint.
- Repeat to the left side.

Teaching Points
- Externally rotate foot and hip as you lift the knee.
- Ensure balance leg turns simultaneously on ball of foot to also face direction of movement.
- Lean body to help transfer center of gravity.
- Lean and react with two-quick steps and arm drive.
- Maintain strong core and upright posture.
- Continue good body mechanics for short sprint.
- Imagine a ball has been kicked, passes, thrown or hit overhead and you're reacting to it in the quickest possible manner with knee-out steps.

Coaches call – lift right knee

Rotate 180-degrees

Variation
- Jog backwards, react to call to right or left side, knee out step, turn and sprint.
- Perform backward knee-out skipping drill and react.

Backpedal | 180-degree Turn | Sprint

Emphasis
- Improve backward movement awareness and ankle stability.

Description
- Begin with backpedal movement, turn to left side by pushing forcefully off right leg and turning on ball of foot in 180-degree movement into forward sprint.
- Repeat action on opposite side.

Teaching Points
- Gently brace abdominal muscles and hold.
- Work off the balls of the feet.
- Keep short steps.
- Maintain same body height throughout.
- Sustain deep breathing rhythm.
- Maintain focus and good body alignment until repetitions completed.
- Gradually increase the speed of movement without loss of form.

Variation
- Side steps to backpedal.
- Forward sprint to backpedal.

Emphasis
- Improve lateral first step quickness.

Description
- Stand tall, feet together, hands by side in a sideways position to movement direction.
- Start off with the leading leg stepping laterally (out sideways) with the toes pointing forward in direction of travel.
- Drive arms as the hip and body rotates laterally and then sprint forwards.
- Repeat action leading with opposite leg in the opposite direction.

Teaching Points
- Rotate foot and leg away from body pointing in the direction of travel.
- Transfer body weight to direction of travel and drive arms.
- Drive rear knee forwards and sprint.
- Avoid sinking at the hips, stay tall with hips remaining square.
- Maintain focus and good body alignment until repetitions completed.

Variation
- Side step x 3 and then step-out and sprint forwards.

FSQA6 Jump, Land and Sprint

Jump

Land, react and sprint forwards

Emphasis
- Improve reaction speed.

Description
- Stand in athletic ready position.
- Jump high off both feet.
- Land and sprint forwards for set distance (ie. 10-20m).

Teaching Points
- Emphasise strong jump and landing position before leading into sprint.
- Keep balance equal between both legs upon landing.
- Land and drive arms rapidly with first step.
- Transfer body weight forwards as you sprint.
- Work off the balls of the feet.

Variation
- Lateral jump (over marker) to forward sprint.

THE BODY COACH

FSQA7: Rapid ins-and-outs

Move rapidly

Stepping in
and out of poles

Emphasis
- Improve forward lateral strength and movement of hip and legs.

Equipment
- 6 -10 agility poles placed 1-2meters apart in a straight line.

Description
- Lead into agility poles at speed.
- Step across and forward through agility poles as quick as possible.

Teaching Points
- Work off the balls of the feet as you transfer weight forward and laterally when stepping through agility poles.
- The step force should be equal on both legs.
- Maintain same body height throughout.
- Keep close to agility poles for quicker speed to end point.
- Maintain focus and good body alignment until repetitions completed.

Variation
- Forward swerve with lateral call to sprint (ie. run forwards through agility poles then on coaches call turn left or right and sprint 10m).
- Lateral running through agility poles.

FSQA8: Rapid Lateral Steps

Step forward laterally   Step back laterally

Emphasis
- Improve lateral strength and movement of hip and legs.

Equipment
- 6-10 Markers, 1 meter apart in a straight line.

Description
- Stand side-on and lead into markers laterally at speed.
- Zig-zag legs forwards and back laterally through markers.
- Repeat in opposite direction.

Teaching Points
- Work off the balls of the feet as you transfer weight forward and back when stepping laterally through markers.
- The step force should be equal on both legs.
- Maintain same body height throughout.
- Keep torso upright and allow feet to work under you.
- Keep close to markers for quicker speed to end point.
- Maintain focus and good body alignment until repetitions completed.

Variation
- Lateral Steps followed by forward sprint (ie. 10 meters).
- Use Agility Poles.

Emphasis

- Improve response to decision.
  Note: Excellent drill for kids in team sports.

Sprint forward

Equipment 4 Markers

- Position first marker as starting point and the second marker 5–10 meters directly forward. Step sideways 2 meters either side of center line and forwards 3 meters and place markers three and four on either side.

Description

- Lead off and sprint forwards to first marker (5–10 meter mark).
- With coaches call (or self-discretion) step to side of call (ie. left or right) at 5 meter mark.
- After stepping at 5 meter mark, travel towards outward marker 3 meters beyond then step again back to run parallel with original starting point and sprint a further 5-10 meters.
- Repeat step with coaches call or self-discretion – left or right sides.
- Teaching Points.
- Work off the balls as you drive arms rapidly and sprint forwards.
- Maintain same body height through-out to avoid disclosing stepping preference (preferred leg to step off).
- The goal is to become agile in stepping both sides.
- Maintain focus and good body alignment until drill completed.
- Gradually increase the speed of movement without loss of form.

Make decision stepping left or right

Variation

- Start drill with 'Falling Start' (FSQA1).

Chapter 5

Reaction Drills (RD)

Reaction refers to the time lapse between the presentation of a stimulus and the first muscular contraction – for example – when a sprinter leaves the blocks. Reaction time can be improved by practice, provided that the practice conditions are similar to the actual requirement of the sport.

When breaking down the movements of each sport, you begin to see various elements that require reaction. In fact, there is a whole range of possible reaction drills for each individual sport in both attack and defense. The following exercises are examples of drills that can be used to help improve reaction. These aim to stimulate your knowledge and understanding for embracing reaction as part of your overall training program. From this, one can add a number of additional sports specific drills.

RD1: Ground Response to Sprint

(a) Lying on stomach

(b) 4-point kneeling

(c) Sitting

(d) Lying on back

Response:
React and Sprint

Emphasis
- Improve reaction time from various starting positions.

Description
- Start in the following positions.
  a) Lying on Stomach
  b) 4-Point Kneeling
  c) Sitting
  d) Lying on Back
- React to coaches call (clap or whistle): i) Raise onto feet and sprint desired distance as quickly as possible.

Teaching Points
- Breathe deeply.
- Keep mind focused on task.
- React quickly to call.
- Rise tall and respond with sprint.
- Drive arms rapidly once raised.
- Continue good body mechanics for short sprint.

RD2: Partner Release

Resist athlete | Release and sprint

Emphasis
- Improve leg reaction, drive and acceleration.

Description
- Place resistance harness on athlete.
- Stand tall in athletic position with coach holding resistance handle.
- Participant drives legs and partner resists lightly whilst moving forwards.
- After a set distance the coach releases the handle and the athlete reacts by sprinting forwards and away over set distance.

Teaching Points
- Maintain upright sprinting position on ball of feet.
- Drive arms and legs rapidly.
- Coach maintains light resistance to allow athlete to travel forwards.
- As coach releases participant, drive rapidly forward maintaining good body mechanics for short sprint.

RD3: Running Starts

Sprint Start
Standing Start
3-Point Start

Emphasis
- Develop explosive reaction from various starting positions.

Description

(a) Sprint Start
- Stand one foot behind from line in a forward lunge position.
- Lower rear knee to ground in line with the front foot.
- Lean forwards and place hands on line shoulder-width apart – thumbs inwards, fingers pointing out with slight arch between index finger and thumb.
- On 'set' call, raise hips into air, straighten arms, lean head over hands and up onto back toes.
- On GO' – explode from line and sprint forwards.

(b) Standing Start
- Stand with favored foot behind line and other leg back resting on toes.
- Arms positioned in ready position.
- On GO' – explode from line and sprint forwards.

(c) 3-Point Start
- Start in sprint start position (see – a. description).
- Raise up into set position and extend arm of forward leg back and up.
- On 'set' call, raise hips into air, straighten arms, lean head over hands and up onto back toes.
- On GO' – explode from line and sprint forwards.

Teaching Points
- Relax and breathe deeply.
- Focus on body position and starting call.
- React as quickly as possible with explosive leg and arms drive.
- Maintain square hips.
- Strengthen core muscles to ensure strong torso.
- Continue good body mechanics for short sprint.

a(i). Sprint start - On your marks

a(ii). Set and Go on call

b. Standing start

c. 3-Point Start

THE BODY COACH

Starting is one of the most important elements in speed development. Previously in First Step Quickness I have detailed moving rapidly off the mark in multiple directions whilst here I will discuss an explosive start for straight line speed, such as the 100m dash, in 4-Stages with 7-Steps.

Stage 1: Preparation

Step 1: Two-steps to leading leg block – dominant foot

Step 2: Three steps to rear leg block

Stage 2: On Your Marks

Step 3: Stand behind the blocks looking directly down the lane. On the call 'on your marks' move forwards and place hands forwards of line for support whilst placing the ball of rear foot onto the block.

Step 4: Place the ball of foot of dominant foot onto front block.

Step 5: Place hands on ground in webbed position with thumb and index finger across rear of line with fingers outstretched – arms straight and shoulder-width apart (or wider) and rear knee resting on ground.

THE BODY COACH

Stage 3: Set Position

Step 6: On the call 'Set' - raise up onto balls of feet, keeping arms straight, the weight shift of the body over the forward leg with the head forward of line, head down, shoulders relaxed, buttocks high and rear leg at approximately 110-degree angle. The weight shift on the front leg allows a quick reaction of the opposite arm.

Stage 4: Exploding Start

Step 7: As the starting gun fires, explode out of the blocks with rapid arm drive, keeping the head down as you drive forwards during the reaction phase.

Key Phases of the 100m Sprint

To assist with the development of speed over the 100m below are 6 basic fundamental phases of the famous Olympic event. Many of the phases vary or overlap depending on the quality of the athlete and interpretation by coaches.

1. Start – Reaction phase (0-10m)
2. Acceleration – Increase in Speed (10-40m)
3. Transition – Lift head up (30-35m)
4. Maximum Velocity – Holding Speed (40-70m)
5. Maintaining Speed – Maintain or decreasing speed (70m-100m)
6. Finish – 100m

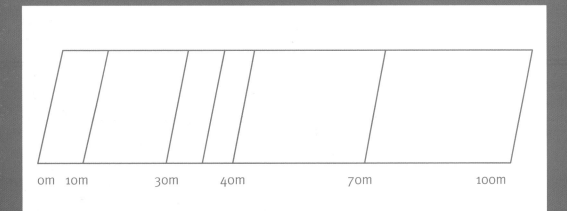

om 10m   30m   40m   70m   100m

Chapter 6
Specific Running Drills (SRD)

Specific Running Drills (SRD)

Specific Running Drills are the most advanced drills to perform correctly. Movement rhythm, frequency of foot strike, balance and coordination and ground impact forces are generally at their highest levels during these specific running drills. As a result, it is very important to work on the ball of the feet during these speed drills to effectively absorb the impact forces. Due to the greater intensity of effort for the specific running drills, they should initially be performed over a short distance in order to maintain proper technique – for example: perform drill over 20 meters. This is because it is far better to train over shorter distances with excellent form to ensure positive training adaptations than it is to work over longer distances with average or poor form. Over time, with neuromuscular improvements one may gradually increase the distance these drills are performed over, as these drills are the most specific to the actual neuromuscular patterns used during sprinting at full speed. Overall, short recovery drills aim to develop muscular conditioning whilst long recovery aims to develop form. For additional drills see Chapter 3 for: (1) Butt Kicks (2) Stiff leg Runs, and (3) High Skips.

Emphasis
- Promote body awareness and development of a more effective running action through various drill variations. This approach is excellent for developing each athletes knowledge, awareness and understanding of one's body position in space and time.

Teaching Points
- Look forward with chest tall and head neutral.
- Work off the balls of the feet.
- Raise thighs of opposite leg parallel to ground whilst running forwards.
- Avoid sinking at the hips, stay tall with hips remaining square.
- Remember, knee-up, toe-up, heel close to buttock.
- Sustain deep breathing rhythm.
- Maintain focus and good body alignment until drill completed.
- Gradually increase the speed of movement without loss of form.

Travel forwards

Slide heel up

Emphasis
- Increase knee lift and frequency of leg turnover.

Description
- Moving forwards raise the knee and thigh up to parallel without the heel of the recovery leg travelling behind the body – like sliding up a wall.

Teaching Points
- Look forward with chest held tall and head in neutral position.
- Work off the balls of the feet.
- Similar to Heel Flick exercise, although thigh raises parallel, heel flicks buttocks and does not travel behind body in recovery.
- Gradually increase the speed of movement without loss of form.
- Be conscious of keeping toes dorsi-flexed whilst wall sliding.

SRD2: High Knees Marching

Raise left knee   Raise right knee

Emphasis
- Promote high knee action and coordination on the ball of the foot.

Description
- Stand tall, feet together and arms in running position.
- March legs up and down in a forward motion raising onto the ball of the foot.

Teaching Points
- Maintain square hips at all times whilst raising thigh parallel to ground.
- Look forward with chest held tall and head in neutral position.
- Maintain dorsiflexion of foot at all times to avoid toes dropping.
- Maintain focus and good body alignment until repetitions completed.

Variation
- Emphasize high knee action using short steps only, landing one foot in front of the other for as many steps as possible over set distance.
- Emphasize speed and distance over the ground.

SRD3: Marching Leg Extension

Raise knee | Extend leg

Emphasis
- Promote high knee action, hip extension and hamstring activation.

Description
- Moving forwards in marching motion raise thigh, extend leg forward and then claw downwards and repeat movement on opposite leg.

Teaching Points
- Gently brace abdominal muscles and hold, maintain square hips at all times.
- Raise thigh of focus leg up above parallel, then extend outwards.
- Use clawing motion of recovering leg to complete sequence.
- Strike the ground with the ball of foot.
- Maintain focus and good body alignment until repetitions completed.
- Gradually increase the speed of movement without loss of form.

SRD4: Single Leg Knee Lift

Lead with right knee

Lower foot to ground, then repeat knee lift

Emphasis
- Improve single leg, leg speed and coordination.

Description
- Lead off with right leg high knee action and arm drive.
- Land raised knee forward of body.
- Fire right leg again and repeat high knee action.
- Continue knee lift of right leg only over set distance.
- Repeat next set with left leg leading over set distance.

Teaching Points
- Work off the balls of the feet.
- Maintain square hip as you drive arms.
- Drive forward leg only.
- Maintain focus and good body alignment until repetitions completed.
- Gradually increase the speed of movement without loss of form.

SRD5: Backpedal

Backpedal | Extend leg back

Emphasis
- Develop hamstrings muscle group and body awareness.

Description
- Maintaining forward body lean, lift left knee and kick leg backwards driving off right leg.
- Continue backwards running action lifting right knee and kicking backwards.
- Continue this action for set distance.

Teaching Points
- Work off the balls of the feet.
- Lift knee then kick leg backwards.
- Maintain same body height and forward lean as running forwards.
- Gradually increase the speed of movement without loss of form.
- Maintain focus and good body alignment.

Variation
- Backpedal to forward sprint – on coaches call.

SRD6: Pure Speed Drill

Emphasis
- Pure speed focuses on running at maximum speed over set distances following by optimal recovery periods of up to 3-minutes before repeating.

Description
- Example Session – 1 x 20m; rest (ie. walk back recovery); 1 x 40m; rest; 1 x 60m; rest; 1 x 40m; rest; 1 x 20m.
- Each sprint has build up of 10m roll-in before maximal effort.
- Rest 5 minutes and repeat set. (Total distance = 360m plus roll-in)
- Ensure the athlete continues running motion to gradually slow down after passing required sprint distance.

Note: Use markers to outline set distances (ie. 20m, 40m, 60m, 80m)

Chapter 7
Mini-Hurdle Drills (MHD)

Mini-Hurdle Drills (MHD)

Mini hurdles are used to develop proper leg action and recovery technique in running. The hurdles themselves act as a tool that encourages the correct leg recovery mechanics – toe up, heel up, knee up. The Micro-Hurdle is 15cm high and used by students and activities involving fast footwork whereas the Mini-Hurdles are 30cm high and used by adults to encourage high knee action. Most importantly, both hurdles are designed to fall over if they are knocked whilst running as a safety element. The hurdles themselves should only be used on a flat, non-slip surface.

The distance placed between each hurdle will depend on the age and size of the participants. In general, a 50cm to 1-meter gap between each hurdle riser will accommodate proper movement patterns. Use this only as a guide and make the appropriate adjustments to suite the participant's age or ability level. Start with a slow speed walking speed to improve technique before adding speed and moving on to more difficult drills. If performing as a group wait until one athlete has finished before the next starts. Over time with regular participation good technique will become automatic.

The following series of drill aim to improve leg recovery speed and the capacity to maintain efficient technique at high speeds.

Athlete and Team Organisation

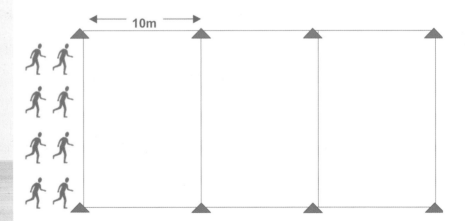

Area
- 40m long and 20m wide (or to accommodate group size).

Equipment
- Markers every 10m – on oval, court or running track.

Description
- Athletes form equal lines across starting marker line. Athletes work from starting marker to set point, specific to energy system requirements.

Speed Training Set-up Variations
The 10m grids can also be used for the 3 main parts of a training session. Each grid provides a boundary and working area that allows training for technique, using equipment, multi-directional drills and sprint work. Example equipment set-up:

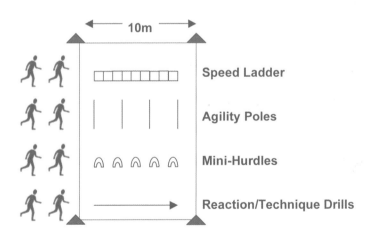

Note: For more details see - The Body Coach® Book – Quickfeet® Dynamic Warm-up.

MHD1: Leading Leg Walk/Run

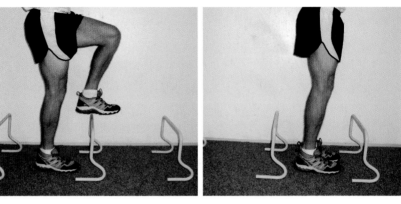

Lead over hurdle with same leg   Catch up with opposite foot

Emphasis
- Develop quick knee lift and effective foot placement.

Description
- Position 6 (to 12) mini-hurdles 50-100cm apart in a straight line.
- Stride through placing one foot over the hurdle with the same lead leg.
- Simultaneously replace the back foot with the leading leg whilst running forwards for two foot placement behind each hurdle.
- Repeat drill leading with opposite leg.

Teaching Points
- Land on ball of foot.
- Raise thigh to parallel.
- Keep toes pulled upwards.
- Maintain upright posture.
- Avoid sinking at the hips.
- Apply good arm and leg mechanics.
- Gradually increase the speed of movement.

Variation
- This drill progresses from walking with speed into a run.

MHD2: Single Dead Leg Walk/Run

Keep outside leg straight   **Cycle inside leg over hurdle**

Emphasis
- Develop quick knee lift and effective foot placement.

Description
- Position 6 (to 12) mini-hurdles 50-100cm apart in a straight line.
- Stand with one leg outside line of hurdles and the inside leg positioned in front of hurdle.
- Keeping the outside leg straight cycle inside leg up and over hurdles.
- The outside leg swings along just above the ground with toes dorsi-flexed.
- Repeat leading with opposite leg on other side of hurdle.

Teaching Points
- Bring the thigh of the inside leg up to parallel.
- Keep toes pulled upwards.
- Maintain upright posture.
- Avoid sinking at the hips.
- Apply good arm and leg mechanics.
- Gradually increase the speed of movement.

Variation
- This drill progresses from walking with speed into a run.

MHD3: Stride Throughs

Single foot over hurdles

Land with opposite foot

Emphasis
- Develop quick knee lift and effective foot placement.

Description
- Position 6 (to 12) mini-hurdles 50–100cm apart in a straight line.
- Stride through placing one foot between each hurdle using an efficient running motion.

Teaching Points
- Land on ball of foot.
- Raise thigh to parallel.
- Keep toes pulled upwards.
- Maintain upright posture and avoid sinking at the hips.
- Apply good arm and leg mechanics.
- Gradually increase the speed of movement.

Variation
- Run through the hurdles and sprint out when reaching the end.
- Gradually increasing hurdle spacing distance to promote acceleration and stride length.

THE BODY COACH

MHD4: Lateral Stepping

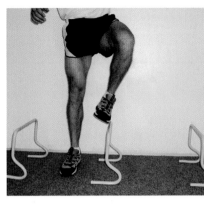

Athlete steps over hurdle laterally

Plant foot and repeat

Emphasis
- Develop lateral knee lift and effective foot placement.

Description
- Position 6 (to 12) mini-hurdles 50–100cm apart in a straight line.
- Stand laterally at the end of hurdles.
- Travel laterally across hurdles with leading leg.
- Simultaneously replace the back foot with the leading leg whilst travelling laterally over hurdles.
- Repeat leading with opposite leg.

Teaching Points
- Land on ball of foot.
- Raise thigh to 90-degrees.
- Keep toes pulled upwards.
- Avoid the feet crossing when stepping – feet swap with each other.
- Maintain upright posture and avoid sinking at the hips.
- Apply good arm and leg mechanics.
- Gradually increase the speed of movement.

Variation
- This drill progresses from walking with speed into a run.

MHD5: Rear Leg Drives

Drive rear leg up and over hurdle   Shuffle and replace feet

Emphasis
- Develop lateral rear leg knee lift and drive.

Description
- Position 6 (to 12) mini-hurdles 50-100cm apart in a straight line.
- Stand laterally and outside line of hurdles.
- Travelling laterally keep the forward (leading) leg straight and drive the rear leg up and over hurdle.
- The leading leg swings along just above the ground with toes dorsi-flexed.
- As the front leg moves up and over the trailing foot lands in its position.
- Repeat leading with opposite leg.

Teaching Points
- Land and take-off from ball of feet.
- Drive rear thigh up parallel and over hurdle.
- Avoid the feet crossing, instead the back foot transferring to the front foot position.
- Maintain upright posture and avoid sinking at the hips.
- Gradually increase the speed of movement.

Variation
- Leg drive with forward (leading) leg.

THE BODY COACH

MHD6: Scissors

Lateral scissors

Scissor with opposite leg forward

Emphasis
- Develop leg and arm synchronization.

Description
- Position 6 (to 12) mini-hurdles 50-100cm apart in a straight line.
- Stand laterally to hurdles with one foot in-between and the other leg outside the line of hurdles.
- Simultaneously jump laterally to the right with scissor action and swap legs in-between next hurdle.
- Travelling laterally drive the arms in time with the legs until the end.
- Continue pattern, then repeat leading with opposite leg to the left side.

Teaching Points
- Land and take-off from ball of feet.
- Maintain upright posture.
- Avoid sinking at the hips.
- Apply good arm and leg mechanics in synchronization.
- Gradually increase the speed of movement maintaining good form.
- Sustain deep breathing rhythm.

MHD7: Two-feet Forward Kangaroo Hop

Hopping

Landing

Emphasis
* Develop body control and power in jumping and landing over hurdles.

Description
* Position 6 (to 12) mini-hurdles 50-100cm apart in a straight line.
* With both feet together, hop over each hurdle in quick succession maintaining good form.

Teaching Points
* Land and take-off from ball of feet.
* Keep feet together.
* Maintain arm angle at 90-degrees whilst swinging by your side.
* Maintain upright posture.
* Keep torso tall and strong.
* Avoid sinking at the hips.
* Gradually increase the speed of movement maintaining good form.
* Sustain deep breathing rhythm.

Hopping

Landing

Emphasis

- Develop body control and single leg power in jumping and landing over hurdles.

Description

- Position 6 (to 12) mini-hurdles 50-100cm apart in a straight line.
- Standing on one leg, hop over each hurdle in quick succession maintaining good form.
- Complete set and repeat with opposite leg.

Teaching Points

- Land and take-off from ball of feet.
- Keep feet together.
- Maintain arm angle at 90-degrees whilst swinging by your side.
- Maintain upright posture.
- Keep torso tall and strong and vvoid sinking at the hips.
- Gradually increase the speed of movement maintaining good form.

Variation

- Repeat drill using left and right legs.

MHD9: Two-feet Lateral Hop

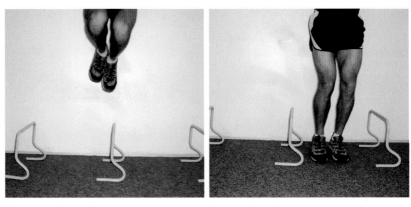

Jump laterally   Land and repeat

Emphasis
- Develop body control and leg power in jumping laterally and landing over hurdles.

Description
- Position 6 (to 12) mini-hurdles 50-100cm apart in a straight line.
- Stand laterally to hurdles with both feet together.
- Drive arms and legs, jumping up and over hurdles laterally.
- Repeat leading with opposite leg.

Teaching Points
- Land and take-off from ball of feet.
- Keep feet together.
- Maintain arm angle at 90-degrees whilst swinging by your side.
- Maintain upright posture.
- Keep torso tall and strong.
- Avoid sinking at the hips.
- Gradually increase the speed of movement maintaining good form.
- Sustain deep breathing rhythm.

Variation
- Jump outside of the line of hurdles.
- Jump with 180-degree twist over each hurdle.

THE BODY COACH

MHD10: Leg-Overs

Lateral scissors

Scissor with opposite leg forward

Emphasis
- Develop leg lift, mobility and tempo.

Description
- Position 6 (to 12) mini-hurdles 50-100cm apart in a straight line.
- Stand laterally and outside the of line of hurdles.
- Moving in lateral direction raise straight leg up and over hurdle.
- Land forward leg and repeat with trailing leg moving laterally along hurdles.
- Continue pattern, then repeat in opposite direction with opposite leg leading.

Teaching Points
- Land and take-off from ball of feet.
- Maintain upright posture.
- Avoid sinking at the hips.
- Apply good arm and leg mechanics in synchronization.
- Gradually increase the speed of movement maintaining good form.
- Sustain deep breathing rhythm.

Chapter 8
Speed Ladder (SL)

Speed Ladder (SL)

Fast feet play an important role in all field sports. Developing fast feet is a skill that can be learnt through the teaching of good running technique. The Speed Ladder drills presented form the basis of learning a wide range of different foot patterns and angles. Through regular practice of these drills improvements in balance, coordination, angling and core-strength are achieved. Most importantly, better timing and foot speed is produced.

The Speedhoop® Speed Ladder is a new multi-directional ladder that teaches athletes about foot placement. Athletes are provided with a number of drills that involve various footwork patterns and angles to work with. As skills are practiced and mastered, the speed, intensity and difficulty can be increased as long as the quality of movement is maintained.

When first beginning, walk through the Speed Ladder in order to learn the correct movement pattern. As time and skill progresses, move into a fast walk or run then perform as rapidly as possible maintaining good form. Start with a few simple movement patterns and master these before progressing.

The Speedhoop® is a revolutionary multi-directional speed ladder that can be manoeuvred into many shapes and angles in addition to the following drills.

For more details go to:
www.thebodycoach.com or
www.speedhoop.com

SL1: Run Throughs

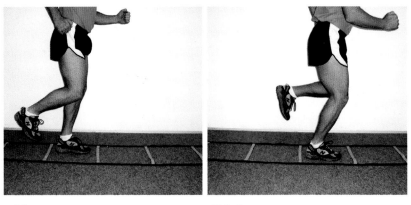

Left foot   Right foot

Emphasis
- Improve foot speed and coordination.

Description
- Run forwards placing one foot in each box with rapid foot and arm speed for the length of the speed ladder.

Teaching Points
- Maintain strong core and upright posture.
- Start slow and build speed maintaining good form.
- Work off the ball of your feet and avoid touching ladder with heel.
- Use arms rapidly in time with feet movement.
- Focus on quality of movement.
- Ensure equal weight on both legs.

Variation
- Complete ladder and sprint forwards over set distance (ie. 10m).
- Complete ladder and add change of direction – step left or right.
- Two feet per box – lead with left leg followed by right along ladder.
- Repeat two feet per box leading with right leg, then left along ladder.

a. Lead in with left foot

b. Catch-up with right foot

c. Continue forwards leading in with left foot

d. Catch-up right foot

Emphasis
- Improve foot speed and coordination.

Description
- Move forwards through ladder placing left foot in the box followed by the right.
- Repeat pattern along ladder leading with right leg followed by the left.

Teaching Points
- Start slow and build speed maintaining good form.
- Work off the ball of your feet and avoid touching ladder with heel.
- Use arms rapidly in time with feet movement.
- Focus on quality of movement.

SL3: Lateral Running

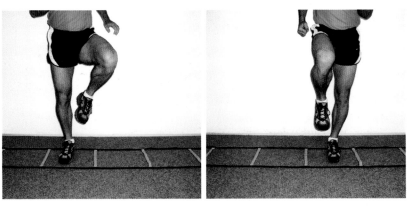

Right foot   Left foot

Emphasis
- Improve lateral foot speed and coordination.

Description
- Stand sideways to speed ladder.
- Raise knee and step sideways into the first ladder box with leading leg.
- Simultaneously raise the leading leg and swap feet by bringing the rear foot into the first box.
- Cover the length of the speed ladder by placing one foot in each box whilst raising the knees up and moving laterally.
- Movement pattern in each box = left foot, right foot or via versa.

Teaching Points
- Maintain strong core and upright posture.
- Start slow and build speed maintaining good form.
- Work off the ball of your feet.
- The trailing leg lands in place of the opposite foot in each box.
- Use arms rapidly in time with feet movement.

Variation
- Repeat action leading with opposite leg.
- Increase knee height.
- Forward three boxes, back one and repeat.

THE BODY COACH

SL4: Lateral Cross-overs

Emphasis
* Improve forward diagonal foot speed and body control.

Description
* Start at the front of the ladder to the left side.
* Enter the right foot into the box forwards at a 45-degree angle, followed by the left foot.
* Then, step the right foot out of the box and sweep the left foot across keeping the foot off the ground.
* With the weight on the right foot, angle the left foot into the next box and repeat above action along ladder.

Teaching Points
* Maintain same body height and let the legs work under you.
* Keep chest facing forwards and arms raised in athletic position.
* Start slow and build speed maintaining good form.
* Work off the ball of your feet and avoid touching ladder with heel.
* Ensure equal weight on both legs.

Variation
* Progress from walking with speed into a fast movement pattern without losing technique or form.

a. Right foot in box

b. Left foot in box

c. Right foot outside box

d. Left foot touch

e. Right foot outside box, left foot in

f. Left foot touch

SL5: Synchronized Lateral Jumps

Land with foot inside ladder   Hop into next box with opposite foot

Emphasis
* Improve lateral foot coordination and synchronization.

Description
* Stand laterally to speed ladder with one foot in box and the other foot behind.
* Using a synchronized hop, jump sideways and simultaneously swap legs forwards and back whilst landing in the next box.
* Complete synchronized jumps along ladder.
* Repeat moving left along ladder; then back laterally to the right.

Teaching Points
* Maintain same body height and let the legs work under you.
* Synchronize leg and arm movements.
* Start slow and build speed maintaining good form.
* Work off the ball of your feet and avoid touching ladder with heel.
* Ensure equal weight on both legs.
* Promote balance and timing between both legs.

Variation
* Repeat movement in opposite direction.
* Same leg, same arm forward whilst jumping.

THE BODY COACH

a. Leading leg into box

b. Trailing leg into box

c. Leading leg back outside of box

d. Trailing leg back outside of box

Emphasis
- Improve lateral foot coordination and synchronization.

Description
- Start sideways outside and behind ladder – with ladder to the left.
- Step left foot forward into box followed by the right foot.
- Step left foot back and diagonally outside box followed by the right foot.
- Repeat action forwards and backwards laterally moving along ladder.
- Repeat movement in opposite direction leading with right leg.

Teaching Points
- Start slow and build speed maintaining good form.
- Work off the ball of your feet and avoid touching ladder with heel.

SL7: Lateral One-foot in

a. Stand outside of ladder feet together

b. Lead trailing leg into box

c. Shuffle sideways and bring feet together

d. Lead trailing leg into box once again

Emphasis
- Improve lateral foot coordination and timing and hip strengthening.

Description
- Start behind ladder laterally – with ladder to the left.
- Step right foot forward into box, then back.
- With each step the left foot shuffles laterally to face new box.
- Continue movements along the ladder to the left side with right foot.
- Repeat movement in opposite direction along ladder with left foot.

Teaching Points
- Maintain same body height and let the legs work under you.
- Start slow and build speed maintaining good form.
- Keep feet light and fast with rapid hip movement.

SL8: Hopscotch

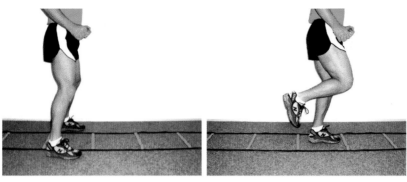

Jump both feet wide   Single leg hop

Emphasis
- Improve foot speed, timing and body control.

Description
- Hop into first box with one leg then forwards landing with both feet wide outside ladder.
- Cover the length of the ladder continuing hop and jump sequence.

Teaching Points
- Maintain strong core and upright posture.
- Start slow and build speed maintaining good form.
- Work off the ball of your feet and avoid touching ladder with heel.
- Focus on quality of movement between hop and jump.
- Use arms to maintain body balance.

Variation
- Repeat single hop movement using opposite leg.
- Double foot hopscotch – both feet together into box, then jump wide.
- Boxer – jump both feet forward into first box, then laterally wide outside first box; both feet back into first box – then jump forwards into second box (feet together) and repeat action – out, back-in, forwards.

SL9: Kangaroo Hops

Hop up   Land forwards and repeat hop

Emphasis
- Improve foot coordination, speed and timing.

Description
- Stand tall with feet together and arms bent by your side outside of ladder.
- Jump forwards into first box with both feet together.
- Continue kangaroo hops, landing in each box for the length of the ladder.

Teaching Points
- Maintain strong core and upright posture.
- Focus on quality of movement.
- Start slow and build speed maintaining good form.
- Work off the ball of both feet.
- Use arms to maintain body balance.

Variation
- Jump every second box.
- Hopscotch – feet in together, feet outside box.

THE BODY COACH

SL10: Single Leg Hops

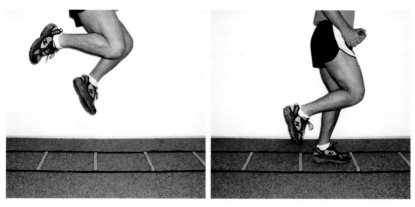

Hop on single leg   **Continue forwards**

Emphasis
- Improve single leg coordination, speed and timing.

Description
- Hop forwards placing one foot in each box.

Teaching Points
- Maintain strong core and upright posture.
- Ensure equal weight on each leg when hopping.
- Avoid hip dropping or collapsing (strengthen with lunges).
- Start slow and build speed maintaining good form.
- Work off the ball of your feet and avoid touching ladder with heel.
- Focus on quality of movement.
- Use arms to maintain body balance.

Variation
- Repeat hop with opposite leg.
- Hop every second box.
- Zig-zag – hop foot inside ladder, then outside.
- Lateral single leg hops – leading leg or trailing leg.

SL11: Speedhoop® L-Drill

Lateral

Forwards

Emphasis
* Improve foot coordination, speed and timing using multi-directional angles.

Description
* Position Speedhoop® into L-Shape.
* Start with lateral (sideways) running motion before transferring into forward run-throughs with one foot in each hoop.

Teaching Points
* Maintain strong core and upright posture.
* Start slow and build speed maintaining good form.
* Work off the ball of your feet.
* Focus on quality of movement.
* In lateral movement the trailing leg lands in place of the opposite foot in each hoop.
* In forward run throughs land each foot in new hoop.
* Use arms rapidly in time with feet movement.

Variation
* Repeat lateral movement in opposite direction – into run-throughs.
* Start with synchronized jumps into run throughs.
* Synchronized jumps into hopscotch.
* Self-exploration – change various movement sequences using L-Drill layout.
* Accelerate out of ladder into sprint.

SL12: Speedhoop® M-Drill

Vary Speedhoop® ladder angles
and foot movement patterns

Emphasis
- Improve foot coordination, speed and timing using multi-directional angles.

Description
- Position Speedhoop® into M-Shape.
- Start with lateral (sideways) running motion before transferring into forward run-throughs and repeat action through M-Shape.

Teaching Points
- Work off the ball of your feet.
- Start slow and build speed maintaining good form.
- In lateral movement the trailing leg lands in place of the opposite foot in each hoop.

Variation
- Repeat lateral movement in opposite direction.
- Self-exploration – change various angles of Speedhoop® and movement patterns.

SL13: Speedhoop® Reaction Response

Start

Response to left

Emphasis
- Improve foot timing and response.

Description
- Position Speedhoop® into U-shape.
- Stand tall with feet together and hands by your side at base of U-shape.
- Lean forward and raise up onto toes until balance is lost.
- Upon coaches call whilst leaning forwards – react to direction of call – left or right side.
- Land and complete run-through on left or right side.

Teaching Points
- Lean and react with quick steps and arm drive into run-through.
- Maintain strong core and upright posture.
- Accelerate out of Speedhoop® into short sprint.

Variation
- Jump and land on spot then into run through on left or right side.

For more exercises see: www.thebodycoach.com
and www.speedhoop.com

Emphasis
- Improve foot coordination, speed and acceleration.

Description
- Space acceleration strips to set distance for longer stride length.
- Start with short fast feet in each grid, moving into longer steps and sprinting action.

Teaching Points
- Maintain strong core and upright posture.
- Start slow and build speed maintaining good form.
- Work off the ball of your feet
- Drive arms rapidly as stride increases.
- Lean body forward with longer strides.
- Land each foot in new box.
- Use arms rapidly in time with feet movement.

Variation
- Lateral steps with step-out into forward sprint – adjust grid distances accordingly.
- Accelerate out of ladder into full sprint.

Chapter 9

Line Hops (LH)

Line hops are introduced to assist in the development of fundamental movement skills. Utilizing a line with various drills helps the athlete co-ordinate their actions with better movement efficiency. Performing quality movement patterns regularly will help transfer these drills into quicker sporting actions by providing the foundation for the development of muscular balance and synergy. The powerful plyometric nature of each drill requires total concentration over the set distances of 10-20m or up to 6-seconds of explosive work followed by optimal recovery of up to 3-minutes.

Line Hop drills can also be used to help identify muscular imbalances in coordination or timing. In effect each drill can be used as a test as well as an exercise for developing strength, speed, reaction and quickness.

LH1: Two-foot Hop - Forward and Back

Stand behind line

Jump forwards, land, then jump back

Emphasis
- Improve foot speed and coordination.

Description
- Hop forwards and back across line using both feet.

Teaching Points
- Maintain upright posture.
- Bend knees, drive arms and maintain deep breathing rhythm.
- Focus on rhythm and timing.
- Maintain focus and good body alignment until repetitions are completed.
- Gradually increase the speed of movement without losing form.

Variation
- Jump in a square formation – forwards, laterally, backwards and laterally.

LH2: Single Leg Hop – Forward and Back

Stand behind line on one leg   Hop forwards, land and hop back

Emphasis
- Improve foot speed and coordination.

Description
- Hop forwards and back across line on one leg.
- Repeat with opposite leg.

Teaching Points
- Maintain upright posture.
- Bend knees and drive arms.
- Focus on rhythm and timing.
- Keep hips square and maintain deep breathing rhythm.
- Maintain focus and good body alignment until repetitions are completed.
- Gradually increase the speed of movement without losing form.

Variation
- 1. Jump in a square formation – forwards, laterally, backwards, and laterally.

Hop along line on one foot   **Bend leg to absorb forces**

Emphasis
- Improve foot speed and coordination.

Description
- Hop forwards along line on one leg for set distance.
- Repeat with opposite leg.

Teaching Points
- Maintain upright posture, keeping hips square.
- Bend knees and drive arms.
- Focus on rhythm and maintain deep breathing rhythm.
- Keep the foot on the line when hopping.
- Maintain focus and good body alignment until repetitions are completed.
- Gradually increase the speed of movement without losing form.

Variation
- Hop backwards along line on one leg.
- Double foot hop along line – forwards and backwards.

LH4: Two-foot Side Hop

Stand next to line

Hop laterally across line on both feet

Emphasis
- Improve lateral foot speed and coordination.

Description
- Hop laterally across line to the left and right with both legs together.

Teaching Points
- Maintain upright posture and equal balance on both feet.
- Focus on rhythm and timing with lateral jumping.
- Keep hops small and fast with arms by side.
- Maintain focus and good body alignment until repetitions are completed.
- Gradually increase the speed of movement without loss of form.

Variation
- Slalom jumps – Zig-zag forwards and backwards along line.
- Knees to chest.

THE BODY COACH

Hop forwards and laterally   **Hop, land and repeat**

Emphasis
- Improve lateral foot speed and coordination.

Description
- With both feet together hop forwards and laterally across the line
- Repeat movement backwards.

Teaching Points
- Bend knees and drive arms.
- Focus on rhythm and timing – aiming for quality of movement.
- Maintain equal balance on both feet.
- Keep hips square and maintain deep breathing rhythm.
- Maintain focus and good body alignment until repetitions are completed.
- Gradually increase the speed of movement without loss of form.

Variation
- Increase knee height.

LH6: Inside and Outside Bounding

(a) Outside Bounding   (b) Inside Bounding

Emphasis
* Improve leg drive and hip strength and coordination.

Description
* Outside Bounding – the foot lands outside normal landing position.
* Inside Bounding – the foot lands inside normal landing position over line.

Teaching Points
* Maintain upright posture with legs working under you.
* Bend knees and drive arms, focusing on rhythm and timing.
* Keep hips square and maintain deep breathing rhythm.
* Maintain focus and good body alignment until repetitions are completed.
* Gradually increase the speed of movement without loss of form.

Variation
* Complete over number of steps or distance (ie. 5 bounds or 10m).

THE BODY COACH

Chapter 10
Medicine Ball Power Drills (MBPD)

Medicine Ball Power Drills (MBPD)

Running at high speed is a powerful movement pattern. Performing specific power drills enables the body to align synergistic fluency between muscle groups by improving strength, power and the appropriate response with the Central Nervous System (CNS)

The ability to maintain excellent body position and running technique over the full distance of the sprint at high speeds is one of the outcomes of proper power training. In addition to the following medicine ball power drills, learning specific jumping, hopping and bounding will assist with body awareness and motor coordination allowing muscles to fire quicker and more efficiently.

Additional drills are available in The Body Coach® Books:
(1) Power Training
(2) Medicine Ball Training
(3) Awesome Abs
(4) Core-Strength

MBPD1: Kneeling Thrust

Start | Explode | Land forwards

Aim: To develop upper body power

Equipment required
- Medicine Ball
- Open area and Measuring tape

Instruction
Kneel on ground across line, holding medicine on chest in both hands. Breathing in, gently lean back before exploding the medicine ball forwards, away from the chest. As the ball leaves the hands, momentum will drive you forwards requiring you to land on both hands in a front support position to absorb the shock appropriately.

Performance Assessment
- Measure distance from starting point to first point of landing.
- Record scores of athletes in a team for comparison.

Start | Squat | Thrust Overhead

Aim: To develop full body power

Equipment required
- Medicine Ball
- Open area and Measuring tape

Instruction
Stand in a squat position with feet shoulder-width apart on a line and arms extended down holding medicine ball between legs. Bracing abdominal muscles, simultaneously extend legs and arms up thrusting ball overhead and record distance of first point of landing. The power of the movement will see the body rise off ground with explosive movement.

Performance Assessment
- Measure distance from starting point (heels) to first point of landing.
- Record scores of athletes in a team for comparison.

Start **Squat** **Explode**

Aim: To develop upper and lower body power

Equipment required
- Medicine Ball
- Open area and Measuring tape

Instruction
Stand across line holding medicine on chest in both hands. Breathing in, gently squat before exploding the legs and body up off the ground whilst thrusting the medicine ball forwards, away from the chest. Ensure you land correctly on both feet with legs shoulder width apart and arms by your side for balance.

Performance Assessment
- Measure distance from starting point to first point of landing.
- Record scores of athletes in a team for comparison.

MBPD4: Leg Curls

Aim: To develop hamstrings (leg) power

Equipment required
Medicine Ball
Coach (partner)

Start

Instruction
The athlete lies on stomach with hands under chin, feet together and toes pointed, whilst the coach stands at shoulder level facing towards athletes feet, holding Medicine Ball in hands in a semi-squat position. The coach rolls the ball down the back of the legs towards the feet. As the ball reaches towards the

Overhead Thrust

calf region, the athlete curls his legs and kicks the Medicine Ball back up to the partner, by flexing the knees. The coach holds both hands up ready to catch the ball, whichever way it travels from the kick, then resets and repeats the drill.

Performance Assessment
If both legs are even in strength, the ball should return straight when curled back. An imbalance in leg strength will lead to the ball being kicked to the side. Adjust accordingly. The partner should be concentrating at all times with both hands raised ready to catch the Medicine Ball. If the athlete has strong kick, the partner may need to move further away for a more effective catch.

Start

Thrust Forwards

MBPD5: Abdominal Thrust

Aim: To monitor the development of an athlete's abdominal power.

Equipment required
Medicine Ball
Open area

Instruction
Lie on ground with legs slightly bent and arms extended overhead holding medicine ball. From lying position, use abdominal muscles and arms and explode up, thrusting medicine ball forwards as far as possible and record distance.

Note: Coach stands approximately 5-10m from athlete to catch and returns medicine ball to athlete.

Performance Assessment
- Measure distance from starting point (heels) to first point of landing.
- Record scores of athletes in a team for comparison.

Chapter 11
Plyometric Drills (PD)

Plyometric Drills (PD)

In extension to line drills, hopping, bounding and jumping using one's own body weight are exercises utilized for improving ground response time and power development. A vertical jump in place aims for gaining maximum vertical height, whereas a horizontal movement focuses on distance from the starting point. As an athlete's strength, skill, posture, power and technique improve jumps are progressed from double leg to more intense single leg movement patterns.

Plyometric Drills are a form of progressive resistance exercise and thus, must follow the principles of progressive overload – a systematic increase in frequency, volume, and intensity by various combinations of exercises. Keep in mind that when one or two of these variables are increased, one or both of the other variables may decrease. Generally, as intensity increases volume needs to decrease.

Perform 3 sets of 6-second explosive movement or loss of form; rest 90-180 seconds between sets. On the following pages are a series of Plyometric drills. For more details see The Body Coach® Power Training Book.

Start   **Hop**

Instruction

1. Set markers 1-2 meters apart over 10-20 meters.
2. Stand behind markers with feet close, legs slightly bent and arms by side.
3. Start with counter movement – squat, swing arms backwards.
4. Hop forwards on both feet, up and over markers.
5. Upon each landing, take off quickly upward again with the same cycling hop action of the legs – use arms for balance and control.
6. Execute the action sequence as rapidly as possible.
7. Work on speed of movement, but not at the expense of poor technique.
8. Maintain good body posture at all times when jumping and landing as quality of movement is paramount over quantity.

Start **Mid-point**

Instruction

1. Start in forward lunge position, arms by side.
2. Simultaneously, bend both knees and lower body then explode upwards in the air as high as possible vertically.
3. At the top of the jump, in midair, switch legs rapidly, changing the legs from front to back.
4. As the body lowers, absorb the shock by flexing the ankle and knee joints whilst lowering the arms – ensuring pelvis remains square.
5. Land, absorb and rapidly jump up again and repeat movement switching legs midair once again, before landing.
6. Maintain good body posture at all times when jumping and landing as quality of movement is paramount over quantity.
7. Repeat drill for up to 6 seconds of explosive movement or until loss of form.

PD3: SINGLE-LEG SPEED HOP

Start

Single leg hopping

Instruction

1. Stand on left leg next to marker, legs slightly bent and arms by side.
2. Start with counter movement – squat, swing arms backwards.
3. Hop forwards on left leg.
4. Upon each landing, take off quickly upward again with the same cycling hop action of the legs – use arms for balance and control.
5. Use the multiple-response action of rapid yet fully explosive cyclic action for height and distance.
6. Perform single leg hop over 20 meters.
7. Maintain good body posture and technique at all times when jumping and landing as quality of movement is paramount over quantity.
8. Rest 3 minutes and repeat using right leg.

Note: Record differences in both legs in terms of time, technique and amount of steps taken over 20m distance. Aim to improve balance between legs.

PD4: ALTERNATE-LEG BOUNDS

Balance on one leg

On go, react and sprint

Instruction

1. Begin by pushing off with the back leg, driving the knee forward and upward to gain as much height and distance as possible before landing.
2. Repeat the sequence, driving up with the other leg.
3. Keep the ankle locked in dorsiflexion and the heel up under the hips to reduce the ground-contact time and promote efficient hip projection upon subsequent takeoff.
4. Alternate arm action is preferred but a double arm action may be used.
5. Repeat movement over set amount of bounds or distance.
6. Maintain good body posture at all times when jumping and landing as quality of movement is paramount over quantity.
7. Bound up to 6-seconds or loss of form.

Variations

1. Alternating single leg bounds.
2. Skip-bounds for height.
3. Skip-bounds for distance.

Chapter 12

Multi-Directional Speed Training (MDST)

Straight-line speed can benefit all sporting pursuits, yet most sports assume a series of multi-directional changes. Tennis for instance, requires forward, backward, lateral and angled speed across the court. Therefore in addition to speed training itself, multi-directional speed training is required that is specific to the sport you play or coach. For optimal benefit, allow optimal recovery time in between repetitions and sets that suits the age group and/or ability level of the athlete or team.

MDST1: T-Drill

Set up markers 5 or 10 meters apart in T-format.

- Run forwards from 1 to 2
- Travel laterally from 2 to 3
- Sprint forwards from 3 to 4
- Backwards from 4 to 2
- Forwards from 2 to 1

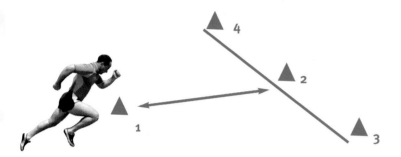

MDST2: Square Drill

Set up 4 markers in square format, 5 or 10 meters apart.

- Run forwards from 1 to 2
- Travel laterally from 2 to 3
- Backwards from 3 to 4
- Forwards from 4 to 1

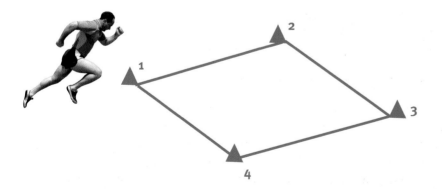

MDST3: Agility Sprint

Set up 4 markers or agility poles every 1-2 meters and the 5th one 10m away for sprint. Run forwards in-and-out of markers then sprint 10 meters. Increase distance for further speed development. Also perform laterally with sprint on left and right sides.

MDST4: Lateral Combo Drill

Set up 7 markers, one meter apart to form a line. At each end place another 2 markers 5 meters directly forward. Place another 2 markers in a zig-zag pattern every 3 meters (total of 13 markers).
- Run laterally in and out through 7 markers, then forwards 5m and through zig-zag pattern.

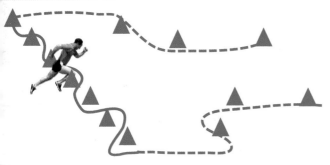

MDST5: Competition Sprint

Set up 4 markers in 10m x 10m square. Walk forward 10m, then inwards 5m and place one marker. Walk forwards from this point another 10m and place two markers 1m apart (total distance, 30m)
Two athletes start 10 meters apart. On go, they sprint forwards 10m then across to the center mark and forwards through the end markers.

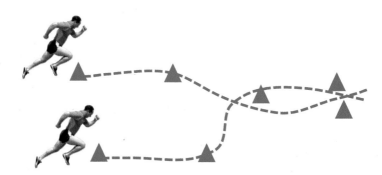

Chapter 13

Resisted Running (RR) and Overspeed Training (OT)

To assist in a runner's speed development, various speed training equipment has been developed that allows similar training resistance effects over shorter periods of time or distances of normal running. These are great training tools for adding variety into a training session and can consist of resisted or overspeed training principles. Always follow manufacture's guidelines when using this equipment.

RR1: Speed Sled

Instruction

A weight plate is placed onto the speed sled to suit the athlete's training requirements. Attach harness around body and secure. Using an open grass area or running track, drive forward in strong running position for set distance of 40m-80m.

RR2: Power Chute

Instruction

Attach harness around body and secure. Using an open grass area or running track drive forward in strong running position for set distance 40m-60m whilst power chute provides resistance

Instruction

The weighted vest has varying increments of weight that can be adjusted to suit an athlete's training age or ability level. Place vest around torso and tighten accordingly. Using an open grass area or running track, drive forward in strong running position for set distance whilst vest adds extra resistance to the running drill.

Instruction

Running stairs help develop leg strength and power. Ensure the surface is non-slip and good footwear is used. Always inspect the area prior to performing drills. Focus on 6-8 seconds of leg drive up stairs of different inclines including stadium stairs. Longer periods will lead to lactic acid build up so ensure full recovery periods. Both individual stair running and bounds of 2,3 and 4 stairs at a time may be used depending on one's training ability.

RR5: Resistance Harness

Instruction

Attach resistance harness around body and secure. Coach stands behind and grasps handle. Using an open grass area or running track, drive forward in strong running position whilst the coach provides light resistance. After set distance of resistance (ie. 10m) the coach lets the athlete go to sprint forwards for 20m-40m.

THE BODY COACH

OT1: Straight Line Overspeed – Bungee Power Cord

Instruction

Both athlete and coach attach harness around waistline. Athlete extends bungee power cord to full length back away from coach between markers. On go, the athlete sprints forwards whilst the coach continuously pulls the bungee cord forwards, ensuring the cord is out of the way of the runner. The overspeed event requires the athlete to adjust accordingly whilst sprinting. The athlete then decelerates after passing the coach.

OT2: Change of Direction – Bungee Power Cord

Instruction

Both athlete and coach attach harness around waistline. Athlete extends bungee power cord to full length back away from coach between markers. On go, the athlete sprints forwards whilst the coach continuously pulls the bungee cord forwards, ensuring the cord is out of the way of the runner. At a set point the athlete changes direction diagonally. The athlete then decelerates after reach desired point.

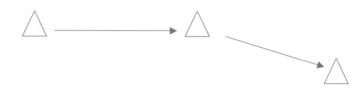

OT3: Downhill Sprinting – Slight Slope

Instruction

Locate a 20-meter gently sloping flat downhill surface of less than 3-degrees that rolls onto a flat surface. A slight slope onto a flat surface ensures correct sprint technique is maintained whilst avoiding any braking to occur (ie. landing on heels). Perform 1 set of 5-10 repetitions with 3 minutes recovery between reps.

OT4: High Velocity Stationary Cycling

Peddling at high speeds on a stationary bike allows you to imitate the leg speed of running without the use of the gravitational forces and stressors of sprinting on grass or the track. Various resistance can be added to support both alactic and lactic acid scenarios – adjust accordingly to your training needs. Apply similar sprint cycles and recovery periods to those on the track with light peddling in-between reps and sets. For instance, performing an 8 seconds sprint with high resistance on flywheel followed by 60-180 second leg turnover with minimal resistance, before repeating as part of 12-minute interval set.

Chapter 14
Speed Training Interval Sessions

Speed Training Interval Sessions

The following activities are examples of speed training sessions that can be implemented to improve speed for sport. Distance, time and recovery intervals can all be modified to suit age, ability, fitness levels and sporting needs. The goal is maintaining good running technique and body posture with each drill whilst running at high speed. All movements should be performed at near maximal effort followed by an extended recovery period, depending on the training objective and outcome, to ensure the athlete is fresh at each running interval.

Sample Sessions Include:

1. Acceleration Runs
Aim: Gradual increase in running speed
a **60m:** 20m build-up and 40m sprint with walk back recovery x 10
   Total Session Distance = 400m plus build up
b **50m:** 20m build-up and 30m sprint with walk back recovery x 10
   Total Session Distance = 300m plus build up
c **40m:** 20m build-up and 20m sprint with walk back recovery x 10
   Total Session Distance = 200m plus build up

2. Downhill Runs
Aim: Run down small flat gradient (ie. 5% decline) in a controlled manner to help improve stride length
• 10 x 40-60m downhill runs with walk back recovery
Note: Always ensure full stride out to gradually slow down maintaining good form.

3. Back to Backs
Aim: Sprint then recover and sprint again
• 4-second sprint, 4-second recovery, 4-second sprint x 5 repetitions with 90-180 seconds rest between each repetition. Complete 3 sets with 3-minute recovery between sets.
Note: Vary sprint time to suit athlete's needs and training requirements.

4. Ins-and-Outs
Aim: Acceleration and speed changes
• 2 sets x 5: 20m lead in, 20m sprint, 20m easy, 15m sprint with walk back recovery (and 3 minutes rest between sets)
• Flying 30's: 2 sets x 5: 10m lead in, 30m sprint, 10m lead out with walk back recovery (and 3 minutes rest between sets)

5. Resistance Training

Aim: Used to increase starting bursts, driving effort and transition of effort from build-up to maintenance.

Equipment includes: resistance harness, weighted sled, tire, power chute, elastic tubing or cord.

- **Weight sled or tire:** 6 x 40m sprints with 90-second recovery.
- **Uphill running:** 10 x 20-40m sprints with 60-second recovery. Rest 5 minutes and repeat set (2 sets in total).
- **Parachute:** 5 x 40m sprint with 90-second recovery.
- Bungee Cord with partner: 4 x 20-40m
- Harness pull with partner: 4 x 20-40m

6. Short Sprint Intervals

Aim: Repeated sprints over set distance followed by recovery

- 5 x 40m sprint with walk back recovery (ie. 90-180 seconds)
- Complete 3 sets with 5 minute recovery between sets
- Total Session Distance = 600m

7. Pyramid Running

Aim: Sprint distances that build up then back down

a   Sprint 1 x 20m; 1 x 40m; 1 x 60m; 1 x 80m; 1 x 60m; 1 x 40m; 1 x 20m with 90-180 seconds rest between each sprint. Rest 3-5 minutes and repeat pyramid set.

b   Sprint 3 x 30m; 3 x 40m; 3 x 50m, 3 x 60m with 60-90 second recovery between each sprint

8. Reaction Sprints

Aim: React to coaches call or whistle to improve reaction time and speed

- 10 x reaction drills (from lying position on stomach) to 30-50m sprints. Allow 60 second recovery or walk back recovery.
- Jump, land and sprint 20m. Repeat 6 times with walk back recovery.

Sprint Starts – reaction to coaches call followed by short sprint effort.

9. Shuttle Runs

Aim: Sprinting over short distance forwards or backwards

- Sprint forwards 10m, then backwards 10m for 10 repetitions
- Rest 180 seconds. Complete 2 sets.
- Total Session Distance = 400m (200m forwards and 200m backwards)

10. Variation Runs

Aim: Sprinting interspersed with another drill

- 6 x 10m Stiff leg runs (BDW7) followed by 30m sprint with walk back recovery.
- 10 x speed ladder stride through followed by 20m sprint

11. Hill Sprints

Aim: Building leg strength and power on hill incline of 10-20%

- Acceleration Distance = 30 meters
- Speed Distance = 40-60 meters
- Speed Endurance Distance = 40-60m or 80-100m. Here the effort remains maximal although the running pace drops towards the end due to muscle fatigue (ie. lactic acid). Hence, ensure full recovery 90-180 seconds before repeating again.

Sample Session:

- 3 sets of 4 repetitions x 30-meters with 3-minutes recovery between sets. Depending on your training objective Active/Recovery Periods between repetitions vary from 1:5 to 1:10
- 2 sets of 4 repetitions x 60-meters
- As the athlete improves, you can add another set (ie. 2 sets of 3 x 60m) or progress the numbers in each set.
- A good alternate to hill sprints is using the Speed Sled or towing a tire.

12. Agility Drills

Aim: Improve multi-directional speed and agility

Lateral Running:

- Move laterally to the left side for 10m turn and sprint 20m forwards; Repeat on right side.
- T-Drill: Sprint forward 10, lateral shuffle right 5, lateral shuffle left 10, lateral shuffle right 5, backpedal 10 to finish.

Diagonal Running:

- Run forward for 10m then across diagonally to left for 20m; Repeat on right side.

Backward Running:

- Complete 4-6 x 20m backward sprints

Proprioceptive Running:

- Run along straight line completing full 360-degree turn over 4 strides to the left then again to the right over 20m.

Chapter 15

Testing – Speed, Agility and Power

Testing – Speed, Agility and Power

Testing of speed and agility is essential in establishing a series of benchmarks to improve upon. These scores can be recorded and referred to throughout the year as a guide to see improvements. The following four tests should be performed on a flat, non-slip surface after an appropriate warm-up. The athlete should wear appropriate footwear and sports clothing. An assistant is required to start, time and record the athlete's performance. Additional testing of core-strength including push-ups, chin-ups and abdominal exercises alike as well as flexibility and range of movement tests performed by a coach are essential as an overall indication of where strengths and weaknesses lie and what areas should be worked on.

1. Sprint Test

Equipment
- Flat surface, Tape Measure and 2 x markers
- Stop watch, whistle and timer

How to conduct the test
1. Record 40m Sprint from standing start
2. Record 60m Sprint from standing start
3. Record 100m Sprint from standing start
4. Record 20m sprint starting from lying position with hands under chin on the line facing forwards

Note: Allow 3 minutes between each test, if performing all four.

2. Speed Agility Test

Equipment
- 3 x markers on flat surface
- Stop watch, Whistle and timer

How to conduct the test
The three cones are set 5 meters apart on a straight line.

- The athlete starts at the middle marker
- The timer gives the signal to start – Test 1: Left; Test 2: Right
- The athlete moves to the left and touches the first cone, returns past the middle cone (start) to the far cone and touches that one and then returns to the middle cone, touching that one.

Note: The timer starts the stopwatch when blowing the whistle and stops the watch when the athlete touches the middle cone. Two tests are performed and recorded – going left and right. The layout can be also be increased to 10m between each marker and time recorded.

3. Standing Long Jump Test

1. Start on line

2. Lower

3. Explode forwards

4. Land and record

Equipment
- Marker and tape measure
- Flat grass surface (preferably, long jump pit)
- Coach to measure distance

How to conduct the test
Stand at marker on line with feet shoulder-width apart. From a static position, squat whilst swinging arms backwards, then jump horizontally forwards as far as possible, landing with legs bent to absorb shock. The coach should measure from the start to the nearest point of contact.

Right foot action

Left foot action

Equipment

- Straight Line (20-30 meters)
- 3 x markers
- Stop Watch and Timer

How to conduct the test

Mark out a 20m distance between two markers along a line. The athlete starts 5 meters behind the starting point at additional marker. Using a jogging lead up, the athlete starts hopping on the left leg from the first marker. The time taken to hop between the two markers over 20m is recorded. The test is then repeated with the opposite leg, one minute later.

      5m jog   **20m hop**

Assess the following areas:

1. Time recorded in seconds for:
   (a) Left leg = _____
   (b) Right leg = _____
2. Time difference between left and right leg hop = _____
Which leg is more dominant – left or right?
3. Total number of hops over the 20 meter distance
   (a) Left leg = _____
   (b) Right leg = _____

Note: Assess difference between legs in time and movement mechanics.

Recording Test Scores: 1- 4
In the table below record your test scores and date of testing:

1. Sprint Test	Time 1	Time 2
• 40 meters		
• 60 meters		
• 100 meters		
• 20m – lying start		

2. Speed & Agility	Time 1	Time 2

3. Standing Long Jump	Jump 1 - Distance	Jump 2 - Distance

4. Single Leg Hop	Left Leg - Time	Right Leg - Time
Time variation between legs		

THE BODY COACH

5. Modified Phosphate Recovery Test

In most team sports, an athlete's ability to repeat short intense bursts of explosive speed are generally followed by a recovery period before another all out effort is performed. In order to measure the ability of the body to replenish the ATP-CP energy system for repeated short sprints, you can perform a modified and refined version of the Phosphate Recovery Test. The Modified Phosphate Recovery Test is an extremely useful test for stop-and-start individual and team sports as well as good method for determining an athlete's speed endurance. In this instance, I have adapted three variations.

Overview
- The test involves performing 10 x 5-second intense sprints every 30 seconds. This method can be repeated for 6-8 second efforts also, every 30-seconds.

Objectives
- Provides information about athlete's fitness levels in terms their ability to recover after speed effort and decrement in performance.
- Provides a baseline measurement early in the season and gauges improvement by comparing scores for an athlete as the season progresses.
- Repeat test every 4-6 weeks to determine improvements and training principles required throughout the season.

Equipment
- Stop watch, whistle and measuring tape
- Numbered Markers – 1-11; plus 2 x plain markers for starting point(s)
- Flat field area of up to 80 meters long
- Person to monitor and record scores for athlete

Instructions
- Establish a start line
- Measure 25 meters from the start and mark the location with a marker = Marker number 1 or 1-point.
- Place an additional marker (x 10) every two meters from that 25-meter mark (Marker 2 = 27m or 2 points; Marker 3 = 29m or 3-points; Marker 4 = 31m or 4-points; Marker 5 = 33m or 5-points; Marker 6 = 35m or 6-points; Marker 7 = 37m or 7-points; Marker

8 = 39m or 8-points; Marker 9 = 41m or 9-points; Marker 10 = 43m or 10-points; Marker 11= 45m or 11-points). Note: Adapt the total number of markers required accordingly to age and ability level – ie. less or more markers.

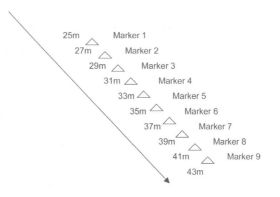

Variation 1: Team sports (start and stop)
1. On the whistle, the athlete sprints as fast as possible for a total of five seconds.
2. Recorder takes note of distance achieved with numbered marker when whistle blows at 5-second interval.
3. The athlete then has 25-seconds to return to the start line. This completes one 30-second sprint cycle. Coach can provide time interval count downs if required to ensure athletes return to starting line on time.
4. The athlete will perform 10 sprints, with a new sprint starting every 30 seconds with blow of whistle.
5. Total test time = 5 minutes.

Variation 2: Straight line speed
In method 2, there are 2 starting points – both 25m from the starting and end points. This allows an athlete to sprint and gradually slow down without braking. The second starting point is in reverse with marker numbers marked accordingly for use in both directions. Apply accordingly.

Note: Whichever variation test is adapted use the same throughout the season to ensure effective feedback. In addition, for team sports, each test can be repeated a second time after a 10-minute recovery period

THE BODY COACH

Variation 3: 10 x 40-meter timed sprint efforts

Using a stopwatch record the athletes sprint time over 40-meters for 10-repetitions with a new sprint starting every 30 seconds. The scoring is virtually the same for variations 1 and 2 and will still result in a percentage decrement.

Scoring of Modified Phosphate Decrement Test

The athletes score will take into account both the total number of markers reached as a score and the decrement in performance as the test continues, as follows:

1. Enter athletes name.
2. Record the score on each of the 10-sprint efforts. If the athlete reached the ninth marker, then record 9 points.
3. Record the Best Single Sprint Score – the highest score attained on any single repetition.
4. Add up all the points to get the Total Score. Note: The total score and the best single sprint score are good indicators of explosive speed.
5. Determine Decrement Scores – the reduction in sprint performance caused by fatigue. Subtract the score on each repetition from the Best Single Sprint Score.
6. Add up all these decrement values to get the Total Decrement.
7. Calculate the Percentage Decrement by dividing the athletes Total Decrement score by Total Score.

Note: All athletes should expect to achieve a decrement of less than 20% if repeated efforts are expected within their sport. For additional variations, 10 x 6-8 second sprints can also be used every 30-seconds. This test may be repeated again after a 10-minute recovery period for more elite athlete for a total of two decrement score variations. It can also be used within a training session as a workout routine for improving fitness levels as will any other short sprint training interval efforts.

Name		Repetition										Best Single Sprint Score	Total Score	Total Decrement	Percentage Decrement
		1	2	3	4	5	6	7	8	9	10				
Paul	Score	9	9	9	8	8	8	7	7	7	7	9	79		
	Decrement	0	0	0	1	1	1	2	2	2	2			11	13.9%

Example:

1. Enter name (eg. Paul)
2. Record each marker score achieved for 10 sprint efforts
3. Record best single sprint score (eg. Marker 9 = 41 meters)
4. Add Total Score from all 10 sprints (eg. 79)
5. Record total decrement = sum of all decrement scores (eg. 11)
6. Percentage Decrement = Total decrement score divided by Total Score (eg. 11 divided by 79, multiplied by 100 = 13.9%)

Recording your test score

Name	Repetition										Best Single Sprint Score	Total Score	Total Decrement	Percentage Decrement
	1	2	3	4	5	6	7	8	9	10				
Score														
Decrement														

Please note: Some level of decrement will always occur if your athletes are giving a full effort on every repetition. If an athlete achieves a zero decrement score, it's an indication that they did not give 100% effort on every sprint or they lack speed itself with an inability to reach a higher number of markers.

Adapted from: Dawson, B.; Ackland, T.; Roberts, C.; Lawrence, S.; "Repeated effort testing: the phosphate recovery test revisited." Sports Coach (Australia), April-June 1991.

Chapter 16

Stage 4: Cool Down

Stage 4: Cool Down

At the end of a training session, the athlete or team should undergo a structured cool-down to return the body to its normal resting state, help reduce muscle fatigue and soreness caused by the production of lactic acid from your maximal muscle exertion and begin the rehydration process.

Ideally, the cool down structure should start with 5-10 minutes of light activity such as jogging forwards, sideways and backwards, skipping or bounding. This should be followed by gentle dynamic stretching drills such as those performed in the warm-up but at a much lower intensity. Once the dynamic movements are performed, static stretching drills are introduced where each stretch is held for between 15-30 seconds.

In the case of team training, where more specific lactic based training has been performed, the athletes need to perform 10 minutes light sport-specific activity followed by light dynamic stretches until their heart rate slows down to its normal rate, followed by some static stretches. If this cool down structure is followed, it is more likely to help reduce cramping, tightening, and soreness in fatigued muscles and will make you feel better as it's a much better way of clearing lactic acid from the blood than complete rest alone.

Cool Down Structure
1. Light Activity (or sport specific)
2. Gentle Dynamic Stretching (refer to warm-up section)
3. Static Stretching

Stage 4: Cool Down – Individual or Team

A structured cool-down is designed to assist in returning the body to its normal resting state and help reduce muscle fatigue and soreness

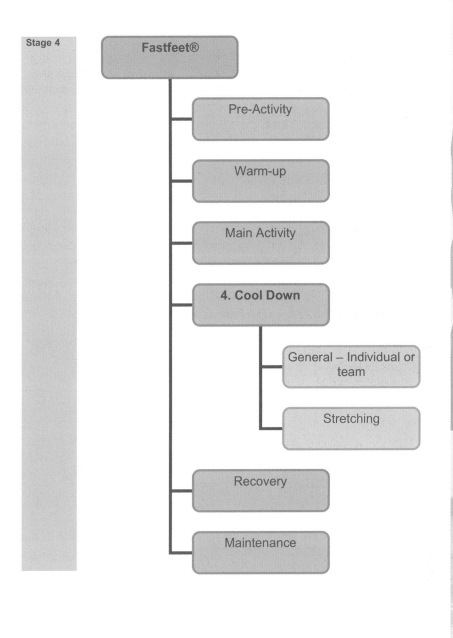

Stage 4

- **Fastfeet®**
  - Pre-Activity
  - Warm-up
  - Main Activity
  - **4. Cool Down**
    - General – Individual or team
    - Stretching
  - Recovery
  - Maintenance

Coach Collins Static Stretching Sequence™

To assist with static stretching drills I have developed a series of static stretching cycles that flow together to ensure each working muscle is targeted. Each cycle follows a specific order of stretches flowing from one muscle group to the next, one after the other. Every stretch is held for 15-30 seconds and the cycle itself can be repeated 1-3 times. Most importantly, adapting these cycles as part of a normal training session will help increase athlete proprioceptive awareness and provide essential muscular skeletal feedback. Ensure an effective cool down has been performed prior to performing the following cycles.

Coach Collins Static Stretch Sequence – Cycle 1

1. Adductors
With feet together, gently push down on knees with elbows

2. Hamstrings
Rest one foot on top of the other with legs straight. Keeping arms straight and fingers cupped extend arms behind body. Gently lean forwards from hip.

3. Hip, Gluteal and Spine
Cross one leg across the other resting foot on ground and gently twist behind.

4. Gluteal
From above (no. 3) release arms, keep legs where they are and lie back lifting legs off the ground. Reach one hand through legs and the other hand outside and grab front of knee and pull legs towards chest and hold.

5. Mid and Lower Back
Release arms and lower legs to ground twisting hips to one side and opposite arm to the other.

Repeat the above sequence (1-5) using the opposite leg to complete one cycle.

Coach Collins Static Stretch Sequence – Cycle 2

1. Psoas
Kneel on ground pushing hips forward. Rest leading forearm across forward high and reach other arm backwards.

2. Thigh
Grab rear foot and pull towards glutes whilst pushing hips forwards.

3. Hips and Gluteal
From above lean to side resting across shins and keeping shoulders square. Straighten back leg and cross behind body as you lean forwards.

4. Calves
Raise into front support position and rest toes on rear heel to stretch calf muscle.

Repeat the above sequence (1-4) on opposite leg, followed by the following stretches (5 –6) to complete one cycle.

THE BODY COACH

5. Lumbar Extension and Abdominals

Lie on stomach on elbows and forearms and gently raise chest off the ground to stretch abdominals and lower back.

6. Thoracic Extension

Kneeling back extend arms forward and hold.

Note: Additional Static Stretches for all major muscle groups can be located in The Body Coach® Stretching Basics Book including the chest stretch performed using a door frame (as shown).

Chapter 17
Stage 5: Recovery

Stage 5: Recovery

One of the most important elements an athlete needs to consider after a training session and prior to the next is 'recovery'. How quickly the body adapts to the last training workload and is able to prepare itself for the next plays a crucial role in determining one's performance levels. Incorporating recovery activities into the training program aims to reduce physical, mental and neurological fatigue whilst accelerating recovery, thus increasing the adaptation time of the body in preparation for the next training session.

Key areas include:
* Fluid (hydration)
* Nutrition
* Massage and Hydrotherapy
* Spinal Unloading
* Sleep
* Meditation

Fluids

A highly intense speed training program can cause rapid dehydration and requires regular small intakes of fluid throughout the training session are required. At the end of a training session, re-hydrating 250-500ml of sports drink helps replenish depleted glycogen stores to assist with recovery. A protein liquid is also recommended for quick absorption to reduce any muscular tissue breakdown. Additional water also needs to be consumed in the ensuing hours that follow to ensure full body hydration.

Stage 5: Recovery

Incorporating recovery activities into the training program aims to reduce physical, mental and neurological fatigue whilst accelerating recovery, thus increasing the adaptation time of the body in preparation for the next training session.

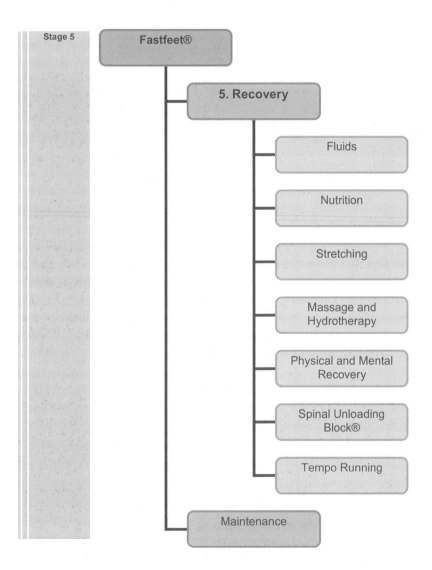

Stage 5

Fastfeet®

5. Recovery

Fluids

Nutrition

Stretching

Massage and Hydrotherapy

Physical and Mental Recovery

Spinal Unloading Block®

Tempo Running

Maintenance

Nutrition

It's important to eat properly and healthy, both before and after sport. Good nutritional planning maintains high energy levels for training and aids in recovery afterwards whilst ensuring a lean body composition. Failing to properly replenish nutrients immediately after training delays recovery and may affect future performance levels. Ensure meals are planned and prepared to avoid any fatigue. I recommend seeing a sports dietician for a nutritional plan that suits your training needs.

Massage

Massage is used to aid athlete recovery by reducing post-exercise soreness, re-establishing full range of motion and enhancing blood flow to tight muscles. The length of recovery time can also be reduced dramatically with post-exercise massage by helping reduce delayed onset muscle soreness. The objective is to increase the athlete's rate of recovery by decreasing soreness and fatigue, speeding up the removal of metabolic bi-products and relieving the increased tension of the muscles.

Hydrotherapy

The non-weight bearing environment of water helps compliment any post-exercise training session by reducing the stress placed on the body and joints. A low-intensity session in the water is designed to facilitate repair by removing any waste products, if applicable, whilst aiming to help improve flexibility by returning muscle to their pre-activity length. In addition, the use of contrast showers (hot/cold) and ice baths and are also used to assist recovery.

Physical and Mental Recovery – Spinal Unloading Block®

Eight hours sleep each day provides an opportunity for the body to repair and rejuvenate itself. In terms of recovery directly after intense bouts of training for the mind and body I'd like to introduce the Spinal Unloading Block®. Lying on one's back with the legs raised has been used for decades as a way of recovery for acute lower back injuries. After prolapsing 3-discs in an accident, I soon learnt of additional benefits of recovery both physically and mentally and as a result designed the Spinal Unloading Block® (SUB). Lying on one's back on the SUB helps heighten recovery of the mind and body with brief 12-20 minute recovery regeneration periods after the cool down phase and rehydration.

The multi-dimensional SUB itself can be turned to suit all limb lengths and soft cushioning allows blood flow to continue throughout the calf region. As the mind and body recover, fluid is re-absorbed into the spinal discs increasing body height once again. This SUB has been very successful in the use of my athletes in all sports. For more details about the Spinal Unloading Block® visit: www.thebodycoach.com

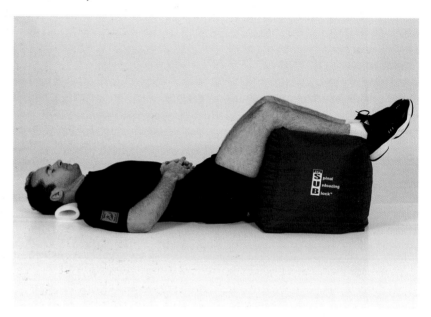

Tempo Running

As speed training cannot be performed everyday due to the physiological demands placed on the body, tempo training (and speed endurance) forms part of a weekly training plan to ensure fitness levels are maintained and smooth running is reinforced. The purpose of tempo training includes maintaining Aerobic fitness, Running rhythm and Body leanness.

Tempo training is performed at a running intensity of between 65-75% of maximum velocity of distances up to 200m. Various body weight exercises (ie. abdominal exercises) can also be performed during tempo recovery periods. It is also important to maintain tempo work throughout the entire year.

Chapter 18

Stage 6: Maintenance

In order to ensure speed improvements are sustained, the maintenance stage is vital in the overall process. Monitoring the athlete physically and mentally as well as muscular screening – testing, troubleshooting, core-strength and power, health specialist assistance including injury management, feedback and periodization action planning ensures good balance is being maintained as part of the recovery and maintenance stages. It's also an essential period that brings awareness of one's body and its responses, attitude to training, sleeping patterns, recovery from injury and so forth as part of the ongoing body management process essential to optimal athletic performance.

Stage 6: Maintenance – Ongoing Body Management

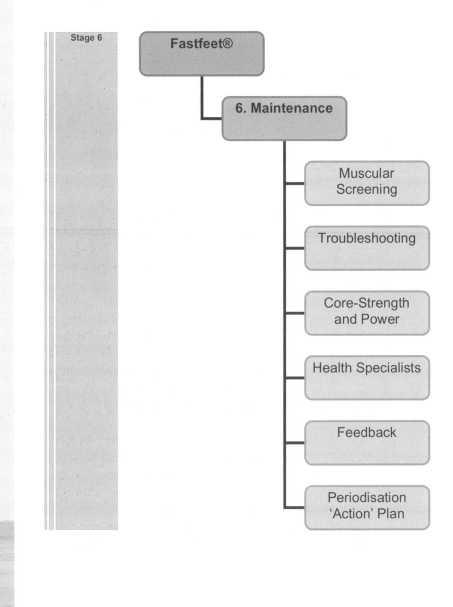

Stage 6

Fastfeet®

6. Maintenance

Muscular Screening

Troubleshooting

Core-Strength and Power

Health Specialists

Feedback

Periodisation 'Action' Plan

Maintenance involves activities and planning that need to be performed on a regular basis as part of the overall training process.

Muscular Screening - Testing

In this chapter, I will draw attention to two basic muscular screening tests that form part of the Collins Technique™ Posturefit® Program. The aim is to draw attention to two common areas of the body to see whether tension or instability arises that can affect efficient movement mechanics required in speed development as well as the application of specific remedies. The two muscular screening tests include:

1. Hamstrings
2. Medial and lateral rotators of the hip

When applying any flexibility or range of motion tests there are two approaches: (1) Muscles warm prior to starting (2) Testing muscles 'cold'. The reason I say this is because the initial aim is to find range of motion in each of the two testing areas by assessing the athlete's limitations – the differences being quite amazing.

The idea is to first find the athlete's normal range of motion and then compare this to when they are warm. This does not mean stretching the muscles, it merely assesses one's range of motion. The one major difference that may arise is when you come across a hyper-mobile athlete, where even when they're 'cold', there is too much range of motion in the joint that requires stability training.

As each athlete is unique, a full assessment of the body, its joints, postural habits and functional movement patterns should always be performed by a physical therapist trained in this area due to a complexity of issues. The appropriate stretch-release and core-strengthening remedies should always be demonstrated and supervised by a qualified health professional to ensure proper teaching technique of each drill is applied and correct pathway for the athlete is adhered to.

Test 1 – Hamstrings Test

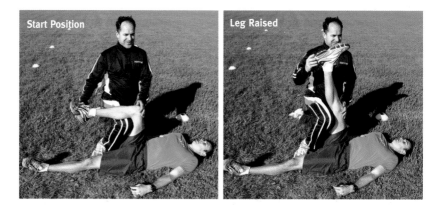

Objective: Assess hamstring length, hip angle and length of back muscles and improve muscle balance.

Outcome: Athletes should achieve 90-degree leg angle in both legs for good flexibility.

Instruction
- Lie on back with one leg straight and the other raised and bent at 90-degrees.
- The 'Coach' (kneeling) rests thigh under back of athlete's knee and holds knee at 90-degree hip and leg angle.
- On "go", athlete extends bent leg up as far as possible without forcing, whilst keeping the opposite leg straight on the ground.
  Note: The athlete's angle from the starting point parallel to the ground. For instance, in the photograph above the athlete reaches approximately 90-degrees from the starting point, which is an excellent range.
- Repeat test on opposite leg and record angle achieved.

Note: Perform test in cold and warm environments.

Sit and Reach

Objective: Coach assesses hip angle and curvature of back when athlete reaches forward towards toes.

Once the leg hamstring length has been assessed, as above, the athlete performs a sit and reach test where the coach assesses the hip, lower and mid back positioning. In many instances, such as shortened hamstrings length (below 80-degree angle) the pelvis can be seen to tilt backwards and actual flexibility in reaching the toes is achieved through extensive upper back flexibility. Normal flexibility in this instance would be seen with natural curvature of the spine with the pelvis positioned at 90-degrees. In a gymnast or diver for instance, this test maybe seen as invalid due to the extensive range of mobility with the torso resting against the thigh when reaching forwards. In most instances, the initial hamstrings test provides the indicator of what will generally occur in a sit and reach test – in terms of hip, lower and upper back flexibility.

Athlete reaches forward

Remedy 1 – Poor Hamstrings Flexibility

For athletes with poor hamstrings flexibility and or a rounded back you need to initiate the following hamstrings stretches without curving the spine to avoid rounding of the back.

1. Kneeling Hamstrings
Kneel on ground and extend one leg forward. Pull toes back, place hands on thigh and keep chest high as you gently lean forwards. Hold 15-30 seconds. Repeat opposite leg.

2. Hamstrings
Rest one foot on top of the other with legs straight. Keeping arms straight and fingers cupped, extend arms behind body. Gently lean forwards from hip. Hold 15-30 seconds. Repeat opposite leg.

3. PNF Hamstrings Stretch
The athlete lies on the ground with one leg raised. The coach gently holds the knee and foot whilst resting heel against shoulder. On go, the athlete pushes the leg away from the body and the coach resists for 3 sets of 6-seconds. Repeat opposite leg.

Other stretches to assist the hamstrings include: Adductors, lower back and pelvic mobility drills.

THE BODY COACH

Remedy 2 –
Weak, Overstretched or Hyper-mobile Hamstrings Region

Weak or overstretched hamstrings can cause muscle imbalance between the thigh and hamstrings muscles that can often lead to hamstring tears when under stressful situations such as competition, as opposed to normal training situations. This is because the only true way to really gauge your progress is in a competitive environment. In the instance of hyper-mobility occurring at the knee joint of an athlete (extending beyond 90-degrees when performing the hamstrings test), attention is also required. Hence, the importance of testing agonist and antagonist strength ratio and flexibility for ensuring muscle balance.

Start

Note: Also see Medicine ball exercise MBPD 4: Leg Curls for improving strength and power of the hamstrings.

Mid-Point

Stationary Lunge

Instruction
Stand in forward lunge position with front foot flat and leg slightly bent and back leg straight resting on toes. With hands on waist, breathe in as you lower rear knee to the ground and breathe out as you rise. Repeat opposite leg.

Variations: (1) Alternate leg lunges (2) Walking lunges (3) Stair walking (4) Resistance drills. See The Body Coach® *Functional Fitness* Book.

Hamstrings Bridge

Start   Mid-Point

Instruction

Lie on back with legs bent, feet together resting on heels and arms by your side. Raise hips up until body is in straight line from shoulders to knees, then lower. Keep heels close to the body for more effective workout.

Variation:

1. Extend one leg and raise on single leg
2. Start with heels raised on bench

Supported Single Leg Squat

Instruction

Stand tall next to pole and grip with both hands and extend one leg forward. Breathe in whilst simultaneously bending the hip, knee and ankles and lowering the body until 90 degree knee angle. Breathing out, raise up to start position. Maintain neutral balance through shoulder, knees and feet. Use pole to support with raising until stronger. Repeat opposite leg.

Start   Mid-Point

Test 2 – Medial and Lateral Rotators of the Hip

1A: External Hip Rotation

1B: Internal Hip Rotation – generally where restrictions lie in sprinters

Objective: Assess internal and external rotation of hip and improve muscle balance and becoming tension free in the gluteal region.

Instruction – 1A and 1B:
- Lie on back with one leg straight and the other raised and bent at 90 degrees.
- Coach (standing) holds knee and ankle for support at 90-degree angle at hip and leg.
- 1A: Keeping the thigh vertical, the partner turns lower leg inwards (external rotation) whilst supporting the knee – assessing angle from starting point.
- 1B: Keeping the thigh vertical, the partner turns lower leg outwards (internal rotation) whilst supporting the knee – assess angle from starting point.
- Repeat both legs and assess angle achieved.

Test Feedback
- Internal and external angles of the leg should be equal in terms of range. For example, 45-degrees both ways.
- Excessive hip mobility requires the introduction of strength-stability exercises.
- Joint or muscle restriction on one side or both requires the remedies on the follwing pages.

Remedy 1 – Strech (Internal Rotators)

Due to the complexity of muscles surrounding the pelvis, in the majority of cases the internal hip rotator muscles (shown in 1B) can become overloaded and protective from heavy training loads, causing muscular tension to diminish elastic nature. Hence, the following stretches help support improving internal hip rotation.

1. Kneeling Sacroiliac Stretch – Start in 4-point kneeling position and hands and knees resting on shins. From here, cross right leg over left and lower down onto forearms keeping shoulders square. Keep leg straight at all times by pointing the toes. To increase stretch, re-position foot of balance leg towards shoulder (in small incremental progressions), maintaining balance position across tibialis anterior (shin). Avoid resting on side of leg as these changes target region. Stretch opposite side.

Other stretches include: gluteal region, piriformis, ITB and TFL. Most importantly when internal rotation is restricted, I recommend regular massage and physiotherapy treatment due to the complexity in balancing this region.

Remedy 2: Partner release

Description: Lie on back and raise and bend athlete's leg at 90-degrees from hip. Place shoulder against knee and gently push across to opposite shoulder. Grip opposite shoulder with hand as you lower for added resistance. Ensure athlete is comfortable whilst breathing deeply. Hold for 5-10 breathing cycles and repeat on opposite leg.

Remedy 3: Gluteal Release

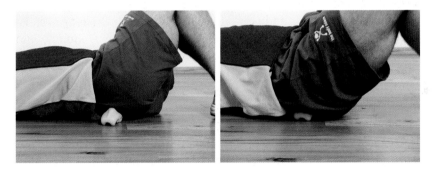

Description: Lie on back and roll legs to the side. Place Muscle Release Tool under upper portion of gluteal (butt) region. Roll legs back over to increase pressure and help release any tension. Using small incremental movements, work around whole gluteal region on left and right sides to help gauge and release muscular tension. Hold position without pain for 5-30 seconds.

Troubleshooting Running Action

Each individual athlete is unique in their running style due to their age, body type and technical skill level. As previously demonstrated in the testing area, various restrictions can occur that may also affect running technique. Either way, there are certain technical principles in running that can assist with better movement mechanics and some bad faults that need to be rectified as soon as possible including postural and foot placement.

1. Running with an arm action across the body with the trunk swinging from side to side.

Improvement: Reduce arm action crossing the center line of the body. Control arm and shoulder movement, making sure they are directed forwards and back. Practice stationary arm swings correctly before running teaches athletes how to relax shoulders and swing arms effectively forwards and back. Also practice at home in front of mirror or via video for better self-awareness

2. Poor head position, causing a hollow back and restricting forward drive.

Improvement: The head guides the upper body movement and good upright head and chest posture is required at all times with the eyes looking straight ahead.

3. Bending from the hips with too much forward lean of the upper body restricting stride length. Or, the upper body leaning backwards with the hips dropped with the athlete being in a 'sitting' position which lacks drive.

Improvement: Stress the correct angle of the whole body. Ask the athlete to make himself tall, keeping the hips high and introducing falling starts and resistance exercises such as resistance harness and speed sled drills.

The Falling Start Drill help pattern the correct body position (lean) for running. It also teaches athletes about powerful leg and arm drive reaction and assists in developing a foot arch for athletes with flat feet (by raising onto the toes).

4. The athlete is not running straight because their foot placement is too wide or their toes are pointed out which over time has them swinging from side to side.

Improvement: Stress bringing the outward swinging leg through in a straight line and a straight forward driving action. Introduce running on a marked line as well as performing the Wall Slide Drill (SRD 1) to avoid overstriding and the Clawing Drill (BRT 7) as shown on the next page.

The Wall Slide (SRD 1) teaches the athlete to let the foot land underneath one's center of gravity and avoid overstriding.

The Clawing Drill (BRT 7) helps athletes learn the proper leg action and foot contact in both legs. Focus on fast foot down action as a fast claw action will follow.

Note: These and other tempo running drills as well as regular stretching, massage, maintaining range of movement and developing good core-strength are required to ensure effective muscular balance and good running technique.

Core-Strength and Power

The fitness ball is a great exercise tool that can be used to improve core-strength and power of the abdominal muscle region. Combined with body weight exercises, the following summary of drills aims to help improve the core region for enhanced speed development. The ability to hold good posture throughout the movement is vital as this ensures a good quality of movement is being maintained. To get the ball rolling, it is important to start simple and master the basic exercise techniques and muscle control required by the body. All exercises should be performed slowly and in a controlled manner in order to effectively target muscles for toning and strengthening.

Core-Strength Routine

Exercise	Target Area

1. Abdominal Crunch – Long Lever

Sets: 3
Reps:10-25
Rest: 30-60 seconds

Lying on ball extend arms
overhead and lower and raise

Abdominal Region

2. Prone Walk-out

Sets: 3
Reps: 10
Rest: 30-60 seconds

Lying on ball walk-out to front
support before returning

Chest, Abdominal, Hip

3. Abdominal Obliques

Sets: 3
Reps: 10-15 each side
Rest: None

Lie on ground with one leg
raised. Bring opposite elbow
across to knee, then lower.
Repeat both sides.

Abdominal Obliques

4. Push-ups

Sets: 3
Reps: 10 -15
Rest: 30-60 seconds

Lying on ball with hands on top side for support. Keeping body tight, raise and lower off ball by straightening and bending your arms

Chest and Abdominals

5. Knee Raises

Sets: 3
Reps: 10 -12
Rest: 30-60 seconds

In captains chairs (or arms extended on overhead bar) raise knees towards chest and lower

Lower Abdominals

6. Lateral Side Raises

Sets: 3
Reps: 10-15 each side
Rest: None

Lie on side of body using upper arms for support on ground and lower arms extended. Simul-taneously raise and lower arm and legs rapidly

Abdominal Obliques

7. Bar Dips

Sets: 3
Reps: 8-12
Rest: 60 seconds

Grip dip bar with both hands and lower and raise until 90-degree angle of arms then straighten

Chest and Triceps

8. Body Dish Holds

Sets:5
Reps: 10 -20 seconds
Rest: 60 seconds

Lie on back with arms and legs extended. Raise up and hold in dish position (banana shape) for set time holding good form

Abdominal Region

9. Collins Lateral Fly™ Series

Sets: 3
Reps: 10-30 seconds each arm
Rest: None

Rest across forearm under shoulder and extend arm overhead keeping body straight whilst breathing deeply. Raise upper leg to increase exercise intensity.

Obliques and upper body

10. Prone Jack-knife

Sets: 3
Reps: 10
Rest: 30-60 seconds

In front support position with feet on ball, draw knees to chest, then straighten

Chest, Abdominal, Hip

11. Medicine Ball Raise

Sets: 3
Reps: 10-15
Rest: 60 seconds

Lie on back with legs raised and arms extended holding medicine ball. Raise shoulders up off the ground and reach medicine ball to toes then lower using abdominal muscles

Abdominal Region

12. Medicine Ball Twist

Sets:5
Reps: 10-20
Rest: 60 seconds

Sit on ground and slowly twist medicine ball from side to side. For power variation throw up and across ball to partner.

Abdominal Region

For more information see The Body Coach®: Core-Strength; Fitness Ball Training and Awesome Abs Books

Strength and Power Training

Beyond core-strength development, power training plays a key role in speed development, namely medicine ball training and Olympic lifting. One must be patient in their development and focus initially on technique and neurological adaptation as a pre-requisite as opposed to lifting heavy. Over time as technique is being mastered through correct planning and prescription, inline with a periodization plan of strength and power training, the necessary action plan for balance will be provided with your speed development and stage 6 maintenance plan as part of the ongoing athletic cycle. Working with a qualified Strength and Conditioning Coach is important for ensuring correct technique is mastered as well as providing a balance of pulling and pushing exercises working all the major muscle groups.

Health Specialists
1. Muscular Screening
2. Posture and Mobility
3. Injury management
4. Sports Psychology
5. Sports Dietician

No matter what your age, a full muscular screening by a qualified physical therapist is essential when first starting out to pinpoint any muscular-skeletal problems that may arise from imbalances or poor posture. Ongoing weekly or monthly check-ups and muscular adjustments and massage by a physical therapist in addition to daily stretching are also recommended throughout the year to ensure effective body management in order to reduce the risk of injury, assist in injury management and maximize speed potential.

To assist with the demands of today's sporting requirements it is also wise to include the assistance of a sports psychologist with the mental preparation of training, competition and maintaining normal lifestyle activities. In saying this, a sound nutritional plan from a qualified sports dietician will also ensure you are maintaining good eating habits and planning, the right calorie and nutritional base for your training and competitive needs. See the leading associations in your country for each profession for guidance.

Feedback

Every athlete, from the beginner to World Champion has a coach whose role is to guide the athlete and provide ongoing feedback on their training and performance. The following points of competence in Coach's Corner (Fastfeet® Speed Assessment) as well as various training guidelines throughout Speed for Sport enable you to grow and improve your knowledge and understanding in the area of speed development as an athlete and coach. The aim is to provide constructive feedback in a positive manner that allows each athlete to have fun whilst growing and developing and wanting to come back for more.

Periodization Action Plan

Periodization refers to an annual training action plan that consists of three major phases:

1. Preparatory (or pre-season)
2. Competitive (or in-season)
3. Transition (or off-season)

The three phases allow the athlete to build, adapt, adjust and improve motor skills, fitness, strength, power and technique for various peak periods throughout the competitive year. Each training phase is subdivided into smaller phases termed macrocycles and microcycles that accommodate monthly, weekly and daily training plans of speed, fitness, power workouts and recovery.

By progressively planning more specific training programs incorporating speed, fitness, power and skill, you enable continuous improvements of physical potential from year to year. Most importantly you are able to monitor your training loads and adapt accordingly. For this reason, I recommend working with a qualified Strength and Conditioning Coach in developing an annual periodization action plan including daily, weekly and monthly cycles and training loads.

COACH'S CORNER

Fastfeet® Speed Assessment

As a speed coach it is important to ensure you are able to address each skill-set with athletes in all areas of speed development. To assist with this development, the following Body Coach® Fastfeet® Speed Assessment guidelines are designed to cover various elements for use in determining being competent. Work through each element when working with athletes. Space is provide for adding additional competencies:

Fastfeet® Speed Assessment

Skill	Outcomes	Competent
Starting	• Can perform a standing start using correct set up and ready position.	
	• Shows correct body position when ready to accelerate.	
	• Demonstrates sufficient balance for set time in standing start position.	
	• Shows correct set up of three point stance starting position.	
	• Demonstrates correct use of arms, legs and body position in three point stance.	
	• Can demonstrate correct set up of couch start position.	
	• Can show set position of crouch start achieving correct angles for acceleration.	
	• Shows necessary balance in set position.	
	• See running starts RD3 and RD4 (Chapter 5)	

Skill	Outcomes	Competent
Acceleration	• Can accelerate and react sufficiently using correct running mechanics. • Shows confidence in accelerating quickly from a variety of starting positions. • Demonstrates good body positions with vigorous and correct use of arms and legs when accelerating.	
Sprinting	• Demonstrates correct arm stroke while running at maximum speed. • Shows relaxed upright posture. • Demonstrates necessary leg mechanics at maximum speed. • Can show correct foot contact in relation to center of gravity when sprinting. • See Running Technique Table (Chapter 3)	
Drills	• Can show teaching steps to develop learning ability of running drills. • Correct use of arms while performing drills. • Can perform high knee drill. • Can demonstrate correct execution of skip, marching and similar running drills. • Can identify and correct faults in running drills.	
Warm Up and Cool Down	• Can perform dynamic warm up exercises using correct postures and range of movement.	

Skill	Outcomes	Competent
	• Demonstrates an ability to conduct dynamic individual and group warm up sessions	
	• Can list the advantages and disadvantages of static and dynamic stretches and warm ups.	
	• Can perform static stretches for each identified body part (cool down).	
Plyometrics	• Identifies the risks and benefits in performing plyometric activities.	
	• Can classify different plyometric activities and apply them in the correct setting for maximum safety and benefit.	
	• Demonstrates correct take-off and landing techniques for various plyometric activities.	
	• Shows an ability to jump and land correctly over mini hurdles.	
	• Can perform take off and landing safely on single and double leg.	
	• Shows correct use of arms and body positions when performing plyometrics.	
Agility	• Demonstrates multi-directional explosive movement	
	• Performs acceleration, deceleration and change of direction activities safely.	
	• Demonstrates correct techniques of stepping, turning and various movement patterns.	
	• Conducts agility training session or drills using Agility poles, hurdles, ladders and alike.	

Skill	Outcomes	Competent

Fitness Testing
- Demonstrates an ability to perform various Fitness tests on athletes.
- Demonstrates an ability to perform various fitness tests on athletes with exercises from within Speed for Speed book on:
  - Core-strength
  - Range of motion (flexibility)
  - Medicine ball
  - Speed
  - Agility
  - Modified Phosphate Decrement
  - Plyometric
- Ability to record and graph data and compare to norms.

Recovery
- Can list and describe various methods for enhancing recovery
- Describes how low-intensity aerobic activity can enhance recovery.
- Describes the role of the nervous system in relation to recovery.
- Conducts low intensity session to facilitate recovery.
- Identify and release common trigger points within the musculoskeletal system.
- Demonstrates correct application of recovery tools such as from rollers, muscle mate, foam rollers and stretch bands and alike.
- Describes the role nutrition plays in recovery, pre and post activity.

Skill	Outcomes	Competent
Planning & Periodization	• Demonstrates effective and appropritate use of equipment.	
	• Shows effective use of space when conducting group training sessions.	
	• Can list the safe training progressions for the various physical components of speed and agility.	
	• Can explain the different types of periodization methods and their advantages and disadvantages.	
	• Shows a yearly or seasonal periodized training plan incorporating speed and agility training. (case study)	

Speed for Sport™ Index

Fastfeet® Speed for Sport™ Coaching

Join The Body Coach® Paul Collins, International author and Strength and Conditioning Coach and his team of experts in the Fastfeet® speed training clinics, workshops, camps, seminars and coaching for all sports – Core-strength, Speed and Agility, Olympic Lifting and Power Training

Elite coach's Paul Collins and Ron Palmer (Australian Rugby League team) presenting at the Fastfeet® Speed for Sport Coaching Clinic in Sydney, Australia

For more details visit the following websites:
www.thebodycoach.com
www.speedforsport.com
www.fastfeet.com.au

Photo & Illustration Credits:

Cover Photo: getty images
Cover Design: Jens Vogelsang
Photos: Paul Collins & Peter Green